THE OTHER WOMAN

▲

TWENTY-ONE WIVES, LOVERS, AND OTHERS TALK OPENLY ABOUT SEX, DECEPTION, LOVE, AND BETRAYAL

▼

EDITED BY VICTORIA ZACKHEIM

GRAND CENTRAL
PUBLISHING

NEW YORK   BOSTON

Grand Central Publishing
Hachette Book Group USA
237 Park Avenue
New York, NY 10017

Visit our Web site at www.HachetteBookGroupUSA.com.

Printed in the United States of America

Originally published in hardcover by Hachette Book Group USA.

First Trade Edition: August 2008
10 9 8 7 6 5 4 3 2 1

Grand Central Publishing is a division of Hachette Book Group USA, Inc.
The Grand Central Publishing name and logo is a trademark of Hachette Book Group USA, Inc.

The Library of Congress has cataloged the hardcover edition as follows:
The other woman : twenty-one wives, lovers, and others talk openly about sex, deception, love, and betrayal / edited by Victoria Zackheim.—1st ed.
    p. cm.
  ISBN-13: 978-0-446-58022-9
  ISBN-10: 0-446-58022-8
  1. Adultery—United States. 2. Communication in marriage—United States. 3. Man-woman relationships—United States.
  I. Zackheim, Victoria.
    HQ806.O74 2007
    306.73'6091821—dc22   2006037668

ISBN 978-0-446-69882-5 (pbk.)

Book design by Giorgetta Bell McRee

CONTENTS

Contents

INTRODUCTION

She's the harpy, the Jezebel, the Lorelei, and the bitch. She seduces our husbands, breaks up our marriages, and occasionally manages to win over our children. Who is this creature who arrives like a wrecking ball to devastate our lives and our families? She's the other woman. Girls grow up primping and dieting to defend against her; boys grow up developing their pecs and abs to be enticed by her. And yet who among us has intentionally brought up our precious daughters to become her?

The other woman has the power to throw a wrench into our relationships and, quite often, bring the entire mechanism to a grinding halt. She makes us feel frumpy, old, stupid, and frigid. If we're able to pick ourselves up and muster our self-respect, her existence might also drive us toward feeling empowered and in control. There are wives who want to kill her (some do!)

and wives who not only forgive her, but sometimes pity and befriend her.

Who is the other woman? She is our friend, our sister, our doctor, grocery clerk, or neighbor. Sometimes, despite our best intentions, she is us. And while the other woman may believe that she got her man, she understands that what she has gained may be the most she'll ever get. So she takes what she can, reminded in many little ways of the existence of her lover's wife, home, and children. Because whether the other woman is old or young, straight or gay, religious or non-observant, she must love or lust in the shadow of someone else's mate.

In this anthology, you will meet exceptional women, many of whom reveal for the first time their own experiences as a husband or lover beds down with someone else, or when they, themselves, take another woman's mate into their bed, or when the sexual behavior of someone they love has profoundly influenced their life. Through their vivid writing, you will share their rage and disappointment, and sometimes their amusement and relief.

The notion of *the other woman* is nothing new. In this anthology, Binnie Kirshenbaum writes about the concept of love and marriage throughout history, reminding us that the wife was selected for childbearing, while the mistress was chosen for her passion and intellectual companionship.

We often think of the wife or girlfriend of the philanderer as the victim, wronged by his lustful eye (and other anatomical parts). What we need to remember, however, is that the don't-get-mad-get-even philosophy could have been coined by several authors whose work appears in this book. Connie May Fowler delivers the raucous denunciation every injured woman wants to hear, while any woman struggling to pull her life back together will learn about survival from Mary Jo Eustace, who lost her actor husband to starlet Tori Spelling. And for "the plot thickens" fans, there's Pam Houston's bitingly funny recollection of a lover who not only had another woman, he had *another* other woman as well.

As much as we try to protect our children, they are too often drawn into the vortex created by the other woman. Katharine Weber writes about being a child befriended by her father's lovers and how this affected her life.

A recurring emotion in nearly every essay is deception. In the case of Caroline Leavitt, her best friend (who was also her sister-in-law) became tangled in a dangerous affair and Caroline was there to offer loving support—until she discovered that her own husband was cheating and his sister had known about it all along.

And what if the other woman is neither friend nor villainess, but she is . . . us? It can happen when we're young and impressionable, middle-aged and seduced, elderly and unwilling to let that opportunity for passion slip away. We might be innocent, deceitful, or simply fall hard for some juicy guy and then forget (for that moment or perhaps a very long time) the vow of sisterhood about never coveting another woman's man. And yet, when it happens, when our hearts are driven by love or lust, good intentions and caution are too often jettisoned, right along with common sense. Lynn Freed reveals how, as a married woman, she fell in love with a married man. Being asked to wash his dirty underwear was bad enough; discovering that he had a second lover brought her to her senses. Dani Shapiro was nineteen when her friend's stepfather swept her off her feet and carried her through years of excitement, deception, anger, and the near death of her spirit. Pulitzer Prize novelist Jane Smiley wooed a man who was still in love with a former girlfriend twenty years his junior who had moved on to other loves, yet still gave him phone sex (and other sex) from time to time. Susan Cheever was methodical in her quest: *I looked my best; I turned on all my wit and facility with words. It was my pleasure to make him laugh out loud. I set my charm to stun.* And stun she did—but to what end?

These essays are unforgettable because of their candor—how often are we given an intimate glimpse into the lives of such talented writers?—and because they remind us how quickly our safe and predictable lives can be rattled. Just the thought of the other woman keeps us on our toes. And really, how smug can we be about love, marriage, or relationships when we know that she may arrive at any moment, or be lurking in the wings?

Whether we fear the other woman, loathe her, or live in her skin, I think you'll agree that these highly personal, anguished, and sometimes hilarious essays are a powerful reminder that her story is never dull.

THE OTHER WOMAN

*You have ravished me away by a power I cannot resist; and yet
I could resist till I saw you; and even since I have seen you I have
endeavoured often "to reason against the reason of my Love." I can
do that no more—the pain would be too great—My Love is selfish—
I cannot breathe without you.*

JOHN KEATS
Letter: To Fanny Brawne (October 1819)

NOT ISTANBUL

▼

Pam Houston

Here's the thing about the other woman. She lives inside your head. She may live on the next street or in the next town or halfway across the world; she may be five-two or five-nine; she may be rail thin (never skinny) or voluptuous (never fat). But however big or small she is, however much space she takes up in the world, will never compare to the amount of space she'll take up in your brain. It is there that she will spread herself from wall to wall, eating gift-wrapped chocolates—so many gift-wrapped chocolates that she will ooze into every nook and cranny of your cerebrum, until you won't be able to think of anything else. And if you let her take up residence there, no matter when you cut her off, no matter how hard you try to starve her, you may never, ever, get her out.

Let's say, for the purposes of this conversation, that the other woman lives in a foreign city. Let's say it is Istanbul (though it is not Istanbul). Let's say she is married to the minister of economics (although she is not married to the minister of economics). Let's say she practices a religion that does not recognize divorce. Let's say she and her husband have four children between the ages of two and ten. Let's say that when the man in your life went over to the city that is not Istanbul to visit her, the man who is not the minister of economics hired other men in trench coats to follow them around. Let's say one or another of these trench-coated men approached the man in your life in a coffee shop and told him that the price of a life in the city that is not Istanbul is one hundred dollars U.S. Let's say the man in your life told you this story with an impish grin on his face and his palms raised to the ceiling, like, *What is a poor American boy in love with an unhappily married Turkish Muslim mother of four to do?*

Which brings us to the man in your life. Let's say he is a painter (though he is not a painter), and let's say the Other Woman is a painter, too. Let's say they met at one of those places in Italy or New Hampshire where painters go for a month to compliment each other's paintings and gossip about other painters and after a long day of gossiping about other painters, fall together into bed. Why the painter wants to risk getting himself killed in a city that is not Istanbul for a woman who enjoys lying to her husband and her children and all of her friends and her religious co-practitioners is only one of the mysteries of this whole escapade. But then, why you have fallen in love with a man who wants to risk his life for such a woman is at least an equally compelling question.

Let's say you have known your painter for twenty years. Let's say you met at a student art show when you were both in graduate school and you had an amazing conversation about some artist who has fallen so far out of fashion in the two decades since that night that you can't be sure anymore who it was. Let's say you were attracted to each other immediately but you did not fall into bed together, and now you wonder why. Maybe it was because you were both too young and you knew you would have screwed up your relationship, and maybe fate or God or providence wanted you to wait twenty years so you would be mature enough to see that you really belonged together for the long haul. Or maybe you did not fall into bed together twenty years ago because in those days you only fell into bed with assholes and the painter was not (at least not yet) enough of an asshole to really catch your eye. Or maybe it was because the painter only liked tragic, super-thin (never skinny) women, and you have never been enough of either. Maybe you were too busy noticing the assholes at the art show, and he was too busy noticing the one-legged bulimics who had to sell themselves on the streets of Paris to put themselves through school.

In any case, let's say you were at a party ten years later (and also ten years before now) where the painter showed up unexpectedly and told you a story about the night his father died and that story made you fall in love with him for certain. Why you didn't fall into bed together that night is also a mystery because you were more or less out of your asshole phase by then, and he had already lost quite a bit of hair on the top of his head, and probably couldn't get the tragically thin women to look his way anymore. But let's say that ten years after the night of the party, your father dies and he is the very first person you want to e-mail and next thing you know, you are back in regular touch.

Let's say you and the painter plan a weekend together in San Francisco, SF MOMA and the galleries—you'll drive—and when the e-mail says *I'm just a dog waiting for you to lower the tailgate*, you know that after twenty long years, you and the painter are going to fall into bed together at last. But first let's say you spend two days of a three-day weekend acting like (what you are) old friends. Let's say that when you tell him that being in love with a married Muslim woman who lives five thousand miles away sounds a little self-punishing, he smiles brightly and says that he is waiting for the Other Woman's husband to die, so he can bring her and her four children to the States. When you ask how old her husband is, he says thirty-eight. When you point out to the painter that he is fifty-one, he says, *Turkey is hard on people; I know I'll live longer than he will.*

Let's say that you decide that what is between the painter and the married Muslim mother of four can only be about the illicit sex, and when you ask (still clinging to the safe distance of long-term flirtatious friendship) *Is it about the illicit sex?* the painter says not only *No*, but also volunteers that sex with the Other Woman is not particularly good. He goes on to say (by way of too much information) that the Other Woman doesn't let him do anything her husband doesn't do, and given the constraints of their strict religion (not to mention the fact that they dislike each other intensely), her husband doesn't do very much.

Let's say that when you finally do have sex with your painter, on the last night before you drive back to your neighboring cities, you let him do every single thing the Other Woman won't let him do, and you do several things to him that she has never even thought of. You do it for hours and hours and hours, until the front desk calls to ask if you intend to stay another night. Driving across the Bay Bridge, you stare out at the boat lifts that stand over Oakland's harbor and wonder why, instead of replaying all of the weekend's good food and great sex and long walks down city streets in the misty dark, you are rehashing every single word he said about the Other Woman. Whatever kind of sex they have, she has lodged herself firmly in the four-bedroom house of your parietal, temporal, frontal, and occipital lobes. The wrapper is off the first box of chocolates and she is making herself comfortable, changing around the furniture to suit her taste and draping her favorite scarves over your medulla oblongata. For not one moment do you consider the possibility that, in this scenario, the *Other* Woman is actually you.

Let's say the first post-coital e-mail is full of words like *wow* and *wonderful*, but in the third one the painter admits that he has *not been able to emerge from the throes of angst regarding the Istanbul situation*. Let's say that this surprises you a little because in the four years since they started sleeping together, the painter and the Other Woman have seen each other three times for a total of eleven days.

Let's say you decide that the throes of angst are possibly the most unsexy place a man can claim to be, so you ignore the throes entirely and send a suggestive e-mail inviting the painter to your favorite fireplace hotel on the Mendocino Coast. When he turns you down politely, even a little condescendingly, you go to Mendocino anyway and pick up a twenty-nine-year-old professional salmon fisherman with lots of hair, great freckles, and callused hands, and the two of you spend the whole weekend in the fireplace hotel's king-sized bed. When the painter pops back up on your e-mail a month later, apparently post-throes and wanting to see you, you wait three days, and then agree.

You have known the painter for twenty years, after all, and you convince yourself that in all that time he has to have had some therapy. Surely it will be obvious to him that *you*—a living, breathing, financially secure, ESPN-watching, blow job–giving (the painter calls them *birthday jobs*), gourmet-cooking, age-appropriate woman with blue eyes and sexy calves who is right there in his own country with her arms open wide—is far preferable to a woman who runs around dingy Turkish hotel rooms screaming *I'm a motel whore, I'm a motel whore* whenever the painter tries to give her a foot rub. And let's say that when the two of you finally make it to Mendocino and the painter tells you he loves you (with no prompting whatsoever from you and no reciprocation afterwards), you decide for sure that you are right.

Let's say that two weekends later, in Seattle, the painter makes a big point of telling you that he sent an e-mail to his other girlfriend in yet another exotic locale. Let's say it is Nicaragua (though it is not Nicaragua). Let's say she is the daughter of a Spanish diplomat (although she is not). This is the Other Other Woman, the *other* one he told you about the weekend you finally (after twenty years) fell into bed together, and frankly, you have been spending so much time thinking about Istanbul that you haven't given Managua very much thought.

Let's say that in San Francisco the painter had called the relationship with the Other Other Woman *a lightbulb relationship*, as if you would know what he meant. Let's say that when you looked at him blankly, he said, *You know, on again, off again.* Let's say he also told you that the Other Other Woman's doctor said she was too fat to get pregnant. You tried (at the time) to imagine how fat one would have to be before a Nicaraguan doctor would declare you too fat to get pregnant, and you decided that whatever it might mean, it meant that she was at least fatter than you. Also, he had reported (incredulity creeping into his voice) that the Other Other Woman told him he could do whatever he wanted with whomever he wanted when he was away from Nicaragua, as long as when he was in Nicaragua, he belonged only to her. Let's say you asked him why he didn't believe her. Let's say you asked him why men don't ever believe a goddamn thing women say.

But let's say that back in the present, in Seattle, on the fifth "date" since you fell into bed together, the painter tells you he has written a Dear Juan letter to the Nicaraguan, telling her not to wait for him. Let's say you say, *I thought it was a lightbulb!* Then let's say you say, *Are we ready to have this conversation? Because I'm not sure we are ready to have this conversation.*

Let's say when you say this you are thinking a little bit about the salmon fisherman, who you have very tentative plans to hook up with in Tobago in the spring, but mostly you are thinking about the way a conversation about the Other Other Woman is sure to lead to a conversation about the Other Woman, and since she is already half naked, watching old Doris Day films and throwing candy wrappers all over your corpus callosum and filling up all your subarachnoid space with half-read *People* magazines, you are pretty sure that you don't want to hear what he has to say.

Let's say he says he thinks it *is* time to have that conversation, and let's say he smiles kindly because he can see that you are tensed like a cat, ready to spring away. Let's say he tells you there is no comparison between you and the Other Other woman; that she, in fact, has started dating a Bolivian (let's say) and she wishes the painter, and even the painter's new girlfriend (by which you can only assume he means you), the best. Let's say you smile back, thinking about how in a perfect parallel universe the conversation would be over at this point, but you can feel the other half of it ticking in the air like a time bomb until, finally, the painter opens his mouth and begins to speak.

Let's say the painter says it was his intention to send a similar e-mail to the Other Woman in her pathetic circumstances, in her corrupt country, in her loveless life, but when he tried, he just couldn't do it. Let's say you take a big deep breath and ask *Why*, and what he actually says in response to your inquiry will be the subject of every argument you and the painter have until the end of time. You are absolutely, positively certain that he said *Because I love you more than the Other Other Woman, but when it comes to you and the Other woman, I feel the same way about you both.* You know that this is exactly what he said, because you remember exactly what you said next: *Don't ever say that to another woman as long as you live, even if you think it is what you mean.*

Let's say this is not how he remembers it at all. Let's say what *he* says he said in answer to your *Why* was *Out of respect for the history I have with the Other Woman, the years together we shared.* And you agree that he *did* say that, but later, after he had called her *the elephant in the room* and, well, after you had started crying and screaming. You are absolutely sure that this was the order of things because you remember that you had screamed, *You mean the years you* didn't *share, right?*

Let's say that because you *have* spent the last twenty years in therapy, you don't say, "How dare you tell me you love me, when you love her the same exact way?"

Because you have spent the last twenty years in therapy you say, *Well, I hear what you are saying, but I have made myself way too vulnerable here, and I have lived too long to settle for being second to anyone, no matter how distant, how tragic, or how thin.* When he says, *But you aren't second* and because twenty years in therapy only counts for so much, you scream in his face, *I don't want to be first, either!* There is still no point in the conversation when it comes anywhere near your consciousness that, technically speaking, the Other Woman is you.

What does start to become clear to you in Seattle is that all the things that make the Other Woman seem to you like such a poor, even self-destructive, choice for the painter are the very things that make her so hard for him to give up: the politically powerful husband who will only have sex in the missionary position; the kids weighing her down like Meryl Streep in *Sophie's Choice.* Between her impoverished country and her overbearing husband and her misogynistic religion, there is no chance her paintings will ever make their way into the larger world. The painter will never have to be jealous of the other woman's successes. The onus will never be on him to be there when she needs him. She will never bleed or fart or hurl a Vlasic dill pickle jar across a sparkling American kitchen. Her thirty-eight-year-old husband will never die. She can exist almost entirely in cyberspace and in the painter's imagination. She will remain his constant, excretionless muse.

Let's say you ask whether or not, at age fifty-one, the painter has any twinge of remorse about breaking up a family, and he will tell you in a bored voice (as though he has told you again and again, though he has *not* told you again and again) that *the marriage has been dead for years.* But if the marriage has been dead for years, you wonder, what is with the men in the trench coats? If the marriage has been dead for years, why don't she and the kids move to the States right now? Let's say he has no answer, but does say, in a fit of frustration, *I can't just abandon her; she risked her life for me.* And let's say you narrow your eyes and say, *She didn't risk her life for you, you fucking idiot; if she risked her life for you for four straight years, she'd be dead.* You are glad that you and the painter are finally, after all these years, really getting to know each other. You feel momentarily happy to live in America, a country where, for all its other shortcomings, women can say such things to the men in their lives and not be beheaded, or boiled in oil, or given thirty lashes and locked in a dingy room upstairs; where women have such an outrageous sense of entitlement that we *never* really see ourselves as the Other Woman. In America, the Other Woman is always somebody else.

Let's say you drive the painter to Sea-Tac Airport, even though you are only one day into a three-day weekend. Let's say you tell him to give you a call when he decides which one of you it is he loves more. Let's say a month goes by and he calls and invites you for Labor Day in San Diego. You don't ask about the Other Woman and he doesn't tell you. Let's say the weather is perfect in San Diego, but the weather has shifted inside of you. In the space between your ears, the Other Woman has gotten too big to have children. She has painted over all the windows and hung depressing art.

Let's say a few weekends later the painter says, offhandedly, that he went ahead and sent that e-mail to the Other Woman. He seems particularly pleased with himself. The two of you begin calling her Istanbul in conversation because (let's face it) neither one of you has ever been very good at pronouncing her name. You and the painter start spending more and more time together, but you are never sure if he is really excited to see you. You start to believe that if you could pick up a limp, or an undiagnosable illness, or a childhood where you walked a hundred miles with your ten brothers and sisters (all of you under the age of thirteen) to the Thai border to escape Pol Pot and the Khmer Rouge, then the painter might really love you. The Other Woman visits you nightly in your dreams.

Let's say one day, helping the painter look for his missing driver's license, you stumble onto a photo of him and the Other Woman in some dreary-looking Turkish suburb in front of a cement block wall. She looks nothing like the woman who has pulled up all the carpets from your cerebral platform and laid down fine, snow-white Egyptian marble. She looks nothing like the dark-eyed (if expanding) gypsy, dressed in silken cloth with mirrors that wink and baubles that rattle when she twirls over to her stash to open a new box of chocolates.

In the photo, the Other Woman is wearing Levi's knock-offs and a flannel shirt. The painter is pale and his comb-over is sticking up as if he is about to be struck by lightning. Together, they look as absolutely unhappy as two people can be.

For the entire four years they were (not) together, the Other Woman said repeatedly to the painter in her thickly accented e-mails, "We 'aff to end ziss story," and as soon as something better came along (being practical in the way men often are), end the story he did.

Let's say you look around the room and realize that, at this point, you are the only one keeping the Other Woman company. Some days you think you are beginning to prefer her company to the painter's. It is this thought that allows you to invite her out of your head (whoever she was), to clean up all the chocolate wrappers and bring in a wrecking ball to get rid of all that damn white stone.

Let's say you buy some steaks for the painter to put on the grill, you open a bottle of Sonoma red and flip through the channels looking for baseball. Let's say you slip into something silky and tell the painter if the Dodgers win tonight, he might get lucky. When he says *Birthday job?* you shrug your shoulders: *Maybe.* This is America, after all, where women have the right.

PALM SPRINGS

▼

Mary Jo Eustace

I'm lying by the pool in Palm Springs, nursing my obligatory margarita, when I notice that my husband is nowhere in sight. In fact, I've been losing track of him all day. I do vaguely recall seeing him about an hour ago, but he was on his cell phone, earpiece planted firmly in place, pacing back and forth like a demented receptionist. I assumed he was talking to his agent, but I wasn't really sure. There had been a lot of phone calls since he joined us a few days ago on our little family vacation. Between the extended telephone time and the three-hour trips to the gym, I'd barely seen him at all. Now, usually I don't mind this sort of thing; most often, I welcome it. Being married as long as we have, alone time is actually a good thing. But this time, something seemed different.

First of all, I had been left alone in the San Fernando Valley. I had never experienced a California summer before and I was beginning to feel like I had an egg on my head that was in a perpetual state of being fried. Secondly, my actor husband had gone back to our native Canada to shoot a television movie of the week about some woman who gets hit on the head and then can predict the future. It was the usual low-budget schlock, made for a network with romantically challenged viewers suffering from low self-esteem and minor learning disabilities. At least I think that's what he told me, but I might not have been fully listening—I had been too busy secretly hating him the whole time he was gone. I kept imagining some hot assistant getting him iced lattes and wet towels, while I was slogging it out in our little bungalow with two kids, praying to God that our air conditioner wouldn't break or that the state of California wouldn't drain the world's energy supply.

When my husband did call, he would try and update me on the movie—I think there was some sort of love story and a couple of murders involved—and tell me how great he was getting along with his co-star, Tori Spelling. Apparently, she was fun and caring and much hotter in real life. I assumed this was a good thing. At his farewell dinner party before he left, jokes flew at the prospect of working with the daughter of a Hollywood mogul. Would she be so surgically altered that he'd walk right by her? Would there be love scenes and could he get a body double? The usual juvenile crap. I even suggested he befriend her. "Who knows?" I laughed, it might be good for his career.

But apparently, at the end of the day, jokes aside, Tori

wasn't so bad to work with after all, and things were moving along quite nicely. I guess they got pretty busy with the night shoots because it was impossible to get in touch with Dean. Now, usually I would have made more of an effort, because I did wonder where he was at two in the morning, but I was having a problem sustaining interest. Truth is, I wasn't really paying much attention at all. I was horribly sleep deprived and couldn't focus on anything. We had just adopted a baby girl, three weeks before he left, and, at the ripe old age of forty-three, I was finding it extremely difficult to concentrate without my requisite eight hours of sleep. Throw our active seven-year-old into the mix, and the few remaining brain cells I had were definitely overworked.

Now here he is, back from Canada, and I believe staying at the same resort as we were, but completely impossible to locate. I put down my drink, sit up in my lounge chair, and look around for my wayward husband. I see Jack, our son, swimming in the lavish saltwater pool, not much of a surprise since we had become official pool whores this summer with all our aquatic hopping. I spot our friends a few chairs away, monitoring their daughter as she attempts to drown elderly guests. We had been planning this vacation for months—the two couples, our kids—a time to regroup before we headed into another school year and the grind of an actor's life in Los Angeles. I decide that I should really try and track down my husband and ask our friends to watch my son as I set off to find my missing partner.

I figure I'll head back up to the hotel room and give Dean a call. I can guarantee that wherever he is, his cell phone is not far away. I pick up our infant daughter, who is lying next to me, and breathe in her smell of sun and fresh air. She is growing at an alarming rate and feels solid and safe in my arms. I hold her close and kiss her sweet little face, still caught off-guard that she is actually ours. Before I head back to the room, I consider for a moment throwing on my cute little cover-up, but then say "Screw it." For some reason, I've always convinced myself that I can carry off anything. The more understated (aka broken in) it is, the better. Through the years, there have been many family interventions over my attachment to certain items of clothing—an old striped shirt, a tired pair of boxer shorts, a threadbare Winnie-the-Pooh nightie—and, of course, my inability to let go. I always thought they looked good, and my outfit today is no exception. I'm wearing my blue bikini with a Hawaiian motif: saggy faded bottoms and a top missing padding in the right breast.

I gather up all the required baby accoutrements and head toward our room. On the way through the lobby, it hits me how nice it is to have Dean back home. Three weeks had felt like quite a long time. I had really missed him. Besides, let's face it, this "doing it all on your own" thing is way harder than I had anticipated.

Looking back, it's funny the things you notice just before your life is about to change: nothing. Everything seems fine, quite beautiful, in fact. I am a little tired, though, and I know something is not quite right. The distance between us and the unanswered phone calls have made me feel a little jumpy. But the weather is perfect, the resort is lovely, and I'm sure if we can just locate each other and connect we will be fine.

I get to the room and struggle to find the key. I balance my daughter on one hip, drop the baby gear on my foot, and, for the tenth time that day, wonder why I can't seem to do anything right—even finding a room key has become a stretch. I finally find it and walk into our lovely, spotless room. The sun is streaming through the window and I go over to the balcony to watch my son swimming in the aquamarine pool. I see his blond head bobbing up and down and, for a moment, I feel a sense of extreme sadness. All I want to do is protect him. It catches me off-guard and I quickly breathe in as I hear the door close. It's my husband. He finally remembered where our room is.

"Hey," I say.

"Hey," he answers in a numb tone. I know instantly that something is wrong. He isn't looking me in the eye. In fact, he isn't looking at me at all.

"What's the matter?"

"Nothing," he replies.

I decide to push. "I can tell there is something wrong. Just tell me."

He turns to look at me and then decides on the floor instead.

At that second, I knew. I knew it all. "Have you met someone?"

He nods yes.

I start to feel vaguely nauseous. I turn to the window, as if focusing on the horizon would help. "Is it Tori Spelling?"

I turn around; he nods yes.

My heart stops beating and I have to remind myself to breathe. I want to ask a question but I can barely open my mouth. "Have you slept with her?"

"Yes."

I try and take in the news. "You slept with Tori Spelling?"

My husband is having an affair with Tori Spelling. I'm not really sure at this point if this is a dream or not. This has happened to me several times before. Not where people I know have slept with Tori Spelling, but where the difference between before and after is so huge, so life-altering, that you're not sure if it is really happening.

I look at the drapes, trying to ground myself, and notice they're a really deep shade of gold and made out of a very heavy material. Really more of a winter drape. I begin to wonder what these drapes are doing in Palm Springs. What am I doing in Palm Springs? I'm from Canada and the last time I saw drapes like these were at my friend's house, just after her mother had a nervous breakdown over a kitchen renovation gone terribly wrong.

Then suddenly, before I know it, I begin to laugh. It was all so absurd. "You slept with Tori Spelling? You've got to be kidding, right? Nobody sleeps with Tori Spelling—not by choice anyway."

"We're soul mates," he says. Then, "She loves me uncon-ditionally."

"What conditions?" I scream. "You've only known each other three weeks."

I'm beginning to think he might be serious and I'm not sure whether to laugh or cry, or what my part is in all of this. I'm pretty sure he said he slept with her, which would make sense if he was leaving me. He would need that sort of validation, you know, for changing horses midstream.

"Look, we've made a plan and money will not be an issue. The kids will always be taken care of."

Oh my god. Kids. That's right. I look down at my daughter. "But we just adopted a baby." The phrase *single mother* pops up in my brain. I start to feel weightless as I cross the divide between together and alone.

"I'm not leaving the kids, or the family," he says. "I'm leaving you."

"But I am the family." The wave crashes. Now it's I who stares at the floor. I can't hold in the tears any longer and I begin to sob. It's a sound I have never heard before. It feels so deep and so sad. My knees begin to shake and I start to become very aware of my vulnerability—my daughter in my arms, my terrible excuse for a bathing suit—and I actually begin to worry that maybe it's all because I look fat. Maybe he was undecided and this dreadful bikini just sealed the deal. Why the hell didn't I listen to my family and respond to all those well-meaning interventions? Who knew? A life lesson: Always dress to be prepared for even your worst moment.

Is he talking?

"I think Jack should meet Tori as soon as possible. She's going to be an important part of his life."

And this is when I start to hate him just a little. Wait. Did he say there was a plan? "You made a plan? You two actually sat down together and planned this. You're going to leave me, and then what? We get a divorce and you marry her?"

Then something else occurs to me.

"Isn't she married?" I ask. I think I have found a loophole. She can't really marry him if she's already married to someone else. Can she? Then he brings me back to reality.

"For now," he says.

I try to make sense of it all.

"So, are you going to marry Tori Spelling?"

"Maybe."

I don't know what to do. Without any warning, the man who had been my partner for thirteen years and our sweet little family were slipping away without any input from me. Suddenly, I felt very disposable.

"You know what?" I say, bringing out my trump card. "I'm going back home to Canada. I'm not staying here. You're out of your mind if you think you can do this to us."

Now it was his turn to react. "Are you threatening me?"

I wondered if I was. I wasn't really sure of anything at

this point. All I could do was take a step back and choke out the words that I hoped would make it all go away.

"I missed you. We all missed you."

He looks at me for a beat. I think I see a crack form, but in an instant it is gone. And just when I thought I couldn't feel any more pain, he says, "I don't love you anymore. And I don't respect you." He takes a breath. "I haven't for a very long time."

Wait. Wasn't it just two months ago that he said he'd never been more in love with me, or more proud of how I handled this move to California? Hadn't we as a family cried and come together three weeks before over the adoption of our daughter, a realization of our commitment as a family after so many years of infertility and endless miscarriages? I had left everything behind—my friends and family, our new house, even my career—so that he could pursue his Hollywood dream and ascend to the big time.

But at this point I wasn't sure anymore. Maybe he had never said that, and everything, except what was happening in this well-decorated but seasonally challenged hotel room, had been a lie.

"I think you should leave right now," I cry. "Just get out."

"I want to say good-bye to our son first."

"No way." I feel myself starting to get mechanical. "I'll tell him you had to go back to work on your movie. You're not going to shatter his whole world. Not today."

"Fine," he says. Then Dean does something truly amazing. He opens up the closet and gets out what appears to be a prepacked suitcase. When did he have time to pack? Was that all part of their *plan*? He takes the suitcase and reaches for the baby. Every instinct I have makes me step back.

"Don't even pretend that any of us matters. Just leave." And at that moment, when everything seems completely suspended, the phone rings. It is our son, wondering where I am. I tell him that I will be down in a minute and hang up. I catch a glimpse of myself in the mirror as I am leaving and I can already see a change.

And for some reason, as I am walking out the door, I turn to Dean and tell him that I love him, and that I always will. I don't know why I say it. I'm not even sure if it's true.

I shut the hotel room door and walk down the hall, expecting to hear his voice call my name and the sound of footsteps running toward me. Instead, there's complete silence. Through the windows I can see children playing in the pool and the palm trees bending from the afternoon winds. But inside, it's too quiet. All I hear is the soft hum of the five million air conditioners that it must take to make this resort run. I put my hand on the glass door and push it open to the outside world. I'm surprised to see that it has remained the same, when I have become so different.

I survey the pool. Guests are relaxing and reading, enjoying the last few hours of daylight before the cooler evening air descends. My friends wave to me and I join them.

"Hey, what's up?" they ask. "Is everything okay?"

I think of telling them, but realize if I do, it just might make it real. Instead, I nod and join my son a few steps away. I hug him and notice how golden he has become in the sun.

"Where's Daddy?" he asks.

I take a breath and tell him the first of many lies to come. I hate doing it. I hate Dean for making me do it. "Oh, he just left. He had to go back and finish his movie."

I look at him and search for a reaction. Could he tell I was lying? Did he hear a change in my voice and know that something earth-shattering had just happened? I heard that kids have a sixth sense about these things.

I scan his face for cracks and secrets, but there are none. He smiles and gives me the biggest kiss ever and asks for a Shirley Temple. And for some reason, this is more than I can bear. It is such a normal request—something you ask for when your parents take you to a special place for dinner, or when you are on a family vacation. It was so innocent and so simple, and then it occurs to me that things would not be this innocent or simple for a very long time to come.

HAIL THE STATUS QUO

▼

Susan Montez

Victor wasn't married when I fell in love with him, even though everyone said what I felt was not love but something more akin to a schoolgirl crush or possibly just an attraction to power. He was the school superintendent in a New York City school district, and I was on the school board. For years I had been trying to get his attention. Victor flirted and acted like I was his favorite school board member, but it never went further than that. As for his private life beyond the school board, he was very secretive, yet I harbored a baseless suspicion that he was involved with Jewel Winter, a young teacher at the magnet school.

My confidantes thought this particularly absurd: Jewel Winter. She was at least twenty years younger than he was; moreover, she was beautiful, at least in that waspy, flaxen-haired sort of way; she was from a rich, upstate, old-moneyed family; and she was very intelligent. It was possible Victor could be in love with her, but not likely since he was too practical a man to pine after someone so entirely out of his reach. But Jewel in love with Victor? That was laughable. Jewel could have anyone, a movie star, a Kennedy, and though Victor might be the god of *my* idolatry, there was no way he was Jewel's. As my friend Trudy pointed out, Victor was a short, middle-aged, fuss-budgety Puerto Rican man, and though being a district school superintendent in New York was a good job, he was still, in effect, a glorified city worker; whereas Jewel was a freaking goddess who probably worked as a teacher purely out of a sense of noblesse oblige.

That line of thinking left people stunned when Victor and Jewel announced their engagement. Even I was stunned to have been so right. I thought they were having an affair; I never dreamed they'd get married. Trudy insightfully amended her opinion, "I guess opposites attract." But what she'd said previously had more resonance than her cliché. What *did* Jewel want with him, anyway? The only thing I could figure was either she intended to marry him to further her career or she was marrying him in defiance, to stick it to her patrician parents. The only question was would they be more upset about his age or that he was Puerto Rican.

Whatever Jewel's intentions were for marrying Victor (I doubted love figured into it), I was at a loss as to what I should do with my own feelings. Aside from being in the grip of raging jealousy, I didn't know what to do with my love for him. I had loved him for so many years; how was

I supposed to just stop? But since he was getting married, I felt like I had to figure out a way.

My Buddhist friend, however, said I was wrong. Just because he was getting married didn't mean I had to stop loving him. No doubt she meant this in some Zen way I misinterpreted because I took it to mean I should wait like a spider until the first sign of trouble and then try to break up the marriage, and it wasn't long before the trouble signs started popping up. I could say I felt guilty and immoral for loving a married man while waiting for his marriage to fall apart, but I didn't. In my mind, Jewel had never played fair to begin with. I was a single mother on the threshold of middle age and she was young and beautiful, and, yes, smart, albeit in a conniving sort of way. I refused to capitulate to the limits of age; I refused to let the young win; I refused to have my mortality challenged. I had just turned forty and was not going to lose out on love without a fight. I decided to be patient and willing to go to any lengths.

Victor and Jewel got married in Albany during a snowstorm. It was an evening wedding, and those who attended said it was very nice, but the president of the school board commented that Jewel giggled during the ceremony, even during her vows. Trudy defended it, saying it was a nervous giggle. I laughed and told Trudy the marriage wouldn't last. Brides who giggled during their vows weren't taking the wedding seriously, and if they weren't taking the wedding seriously, they surely wouldn't take the marriage seriously.

After the wedding, Jewel transferred out of the district

and became an assistant principal in the South Bronx. The following academic year she became a principal, the youngest (and, yes, most beautiful) in New York City. Trudy said she was like Victor, a careerist, a workaholic. Mrs. Tejada, however, my Mexican compadre on the school board and maternalesque friend of Victor's, said that Victor had not wanted Jewel to be a principal. He wanted to start a family. I hinted at the starting-a-family business to Mercedes Garcia, who laughed. Jewel was never going to have a baby with *him*, she said. "How do you know?" I asked.

"Woman's intuition," she said. "Besides, Jewel is hardly the barefoot, pregnant type."

They had been married just over a year when Victor and I started having an affair. It started out tentatively. He showed up at my house one night after a school board meeting, and he was forlorn and sad. Obviously he had come to me as a safe haven. From various sources, I had heard that their marriage was embattled from the get-go, but Victor didn't relate too many of the details. He did confide in me that one reason he married her was because he had wanted to start a family. He knew it was a little crazy at fifty, but he'd just never had time for it before. Jewel looked the right age for childbearing. It confused me that Victor had married Jewel for that reason. It was like buying a thoroughbred race horse to do the spring plowing.

Our affair evolved from something that started as a consequence of Victor's marital unhappiness into something passionate and wonderful, even more wonderful than my fantasies had permitted. He began coming over to my house more frequently and we would frolic in divine intimacy, and there was no place I'd have rather been than in his arms. When Victor got a job in Hartford, which was only two hours from New York, he said Jewel was not moving with him, that she was staying in New York (in their Riverdale condo, overlooking the Hudson River), where her career was. Besides, she didn't like Hartford. To her, going to Hartford would be the equivalent of returning to Albany, where she grew up. They would have a commuter marriage. Then he hinted of phasing her out, divorcing her, and, suddenly, I had a panic that without Jewel, I would lose Victor.

Though I loved Victor more than I had loved any man, I didn't want him to divorce Jewel. There were two reasons why I surmised he was mine only as long as he stayed married to Jewel. For one, I was his sanctuary away from her, and two, there was that whole baby issue. Besides, I didn't need him to be divorced. I was perfectly happy with things as they were, particularly with Victor in Hartford and Jewel still living in New York. It seemed to me that all three of us were happy the way things were—or at least we should be. Jewel was busy climbing the career ladder of education by helping young, disenfranchised children, thereby fulfilling her noblesse oblige mission, and she would no doubt be a superintendent one day, then the head of a state department of education or something. I admit I was amazed at how focused and hardworking Jewel was at such a young age.

Theoretically, I would have liked Victor to get a divorce and marry me, but practically I knew I couldn't be married to Victor. He was too high maintenance, with his perfectly ironed shirts and his sensitivity to noise and temperature and anything not done his way. Frankly, I was too lazy to be his wife, which also required too many professional functions and educational galas. But mainly I knew that Victor had never gotten this baby thing out of his mind, and if he divorced Jewel, he would be on the prowl for a new mother of his children. I was already a single parent and past the watermark of ideal mother material. Since I had begun competing with Jewel on the terrain of youth and beauty, I looked damn good, but there was no turning back the biological clock, and I didn't want to have a baby besides. So Jewel was not an obstacle on my road of bliss, but rather a security blanket.

Our affair went on for the duration of their marriage, and though I justified in my mind that everyone was happy (after all, I truly was), I did realize that Victor and Jewel were miserably married. I heard it from Victor. I heard it from Victor's friends, I heard it from people who knew Jewel and had no idea of my relationship with Victor. Still, just because they were miserably married didn't, in my mind, mean that either one of them was miserable, per se. My only fears would come when Victor would get melancholy over not being a father. I hoped it was a regret that would pass with age, and the intervals between episodes of his melancholy did increase, but they never entirely disappeared.

One night when I was in Hartford, Victor and I were

watching TV, fully clothed and innocent in appearance, there was a knock on the door. It was Jewel. Instead of thinking logically and letting Jewel in, saying I had dropped by while I happened to be in the area (attending a conference or something), Victor pushed me into the bathroom and told me to lock the door. Of course, when Jewel came in, having waited to get in to begin with and already suspicious, she went right to the closed bathroom door.

Victor said, calmly, "Let's go downstairs and talk, where we can take a walk." But Jewel was working up to hysteria. She had caught her husband with another woman, and she wanted to know what every woman always wanted to know: Who was she?

"It doesn't matter," Victor said. "It's not what you think."

She was crying and started yelling. "I'll go to the press. I'll wreck your career. I swear to God I will."

I sat in the dark bathroom musing that she might actually love him. I was even amazed that she was demonstrating signs of being genuinely hurt. On the other hand, I couldn't help thinking how funny it was that Jewel was causing such a scene because of me. "Ha ha," I thought to myself, "the older mistress triumphs over the young wife."

"I missed you," she yelled, "and I drove all the way up here in the rain to see you and you've got another woman locked in the bathroom. Who is it, Victor? Tell me who it is."

Then there was a loud bang on the bathroom door.

"Get out of there, you fucking whore. You fucking home wrecker. Get out of that fucking bathroom."

I would have felt sorry for Jewel, but I couldn't help my amusement. I liked the fact I had brought the beautiful, rich, should-have-married-a-movie-star to this vulnerable position (though, granted, I was the one stuck in the bathroom). I liked that Jewel was crying and out of control. I had cried enough when she married him; now it was her turn. I temporarily forgot that I needed Jewel.

She alternately banged on the bathroom door and screamed at Victor. He remained calm and kept asking her to go downstairs with him and let the bathroom occupant leave, but she wasn't having it. She wanted to know who her nemesis was. She wanted to know who was trying to steal her husband.

"If I tell you who's here, will you let her leave and calm down?"

"Yes," she said.

"You promise?" he asked. "You'll let her leave and stop screaming. It's not what you think, anyway."

"Who is it?" she asked.

"It's just Susan Montez," he said, matter-of-factly, which is what he should have done when we were sitting in the living room looking completely innocent.

"Montez?" she screamed. "You told me you hated her. You swore you'd never have anything to do with Montez."

"It's not like *that*," he said.

She slammed the bathroom door with the palm of

her hand. "Get out of there, Susan, you fucking piece of trash. He's my husband, not yours."

At this point, I felt there was a good chance I'd be spending the night in the bathroom. I could hear Victor trying to talk her down, and she would scream or cry until finally there was a modicum of silence. Victor finally knocked on the door and told me I could come out. I opened the door slowly and when I walked out, Jewel lunged at me. Her long hair was in a braid twisted around her head, and she was wearing an oversized T-shirt. I didn't realize Jewel was such a big girl, but I remembered hearing she had rowed crew at her old prep school. Victor struggled to hold her back and told me to hurry, run.

I drove back to New York replaying the episode in my head and philosophizing over its meaning. I should have had some sympathy for Jewel, instead of finding the evening's events wildly funny, but I didn't. I was always so jealous of Jewel, not only because she married Victor, but because she was everything I ever wanted to be. I had squandered my youth in terms of a bad marriage and a haphazard career, whereas Jewel was focused, hardworking, and knew exactly what she wanted and always managed to get it. True, Victor was a lot older than she was, but he wasn't a loser. What's more, I didn't come from tons of money, and though I might be considered extremely attractive, I never had Jewel's beauty. That Jewel had debased and humiliated herself because she was jealous of *me* was hugely funny because it was so ironic, and I reveled in winning the battle against youth. I felt immortal.

For weeks afterward, Jewel stalked me and called my house. I was amused that I had been jealous of Jewel, and now she was jealous of me. It was a condition I savored, while she must have driven herself crazy trying to figure out what I had that she didn't.

The unfunny element was that this little misadventure was part of the fodder that led to divorce. Even though tormenting Jewel was a priceless experience, there was equilibrium in the status quo I didn't want disturbed.

I thought about the documentary I had seen on Jacques Derrida. When asked about love, he said it was about the who and the what. Do we love the individual person, the who, or do we love what they do, the what? I was the who Victor loved and Jewel was the what, and I realized that a man might have an affair with a who, but he would marry a what, and if Jewel were gone, Victor would be looking for another what.

Their divorce was not pleasant for me, and I told that to Victor. I actually pleaded Jewel's case. I assured him that in a few years, Jewel would want a baby, like when she turned thirty-three. Women often turned thirty-three and wanted a baby, and besides, she was the wife he'd always dreamed of having. I tried to paint a swell picture of Jewel, but Victor said, "If you think she's so great, you marry her."

Once they were divorced, things between Victor and me changed. Not that he seemed to love me less, only that he began confusing me with Jewel and accusing me of things, I began surmising, that Jewel had done. In San Francisco, he got miffed at me because he felt it took me too long getting from the airport to the hotel. I got miffed and left the hotel room to have a surreptitious smoke. When I came back, he wanted to know where I'd been, had I picked up a man. He was jealous and suspicious.

"What are you, crazy?" I asked. "I went out to have a cigarette because you were acting like an ass."

Another time, walking down the street in Queens, he stopped and said, "I don't want to have a scene. You're always making scenes on the street." The reality was we had barely begun to frequent the streets together. It was evidently Jewel who had had the scenes, but he had begun confusing us. In my attempt to compete with Jewel, I had started looking a bit like her.

Mercedes Garcia was the one who told me about Jewel giving birth.

"What?" I said.

"Oh, Victor's not the father, but she was pregnant when they got a divorce." Victor had not told me that. What a crushing, ego-shattering event that must have been for him—to have wanted a baby with a wife who shunned having a baby with him, then her getting pregnant with another man while she was still married to him. Our sins seemed rather minor in comparison.

Victor and I continued our affair two years after the divorce. At one point, I almost began to think he had put the whole baby issue behind him. He seemed very happy one particular fall and began driving down to New York three or four times a week to see me. We'd take long walks through the park, go to the movies, and have sex. We always had sex. He also began talking about marriage and retirement plans, and how he wanted to get married again. Though it was hard for me to imagine being married to Victor, I thought he had gotten it into his head to marry me. I was wrong.

One night I called his house and a strange woman answered the phone. She said Victor wasn't home but asked to take a message. "Yeah," I said, "tell him his fiancée called."

"His fiancée?" she said, confused. "I am his fiancée."

"Well, well. I guess he has two fiancées. Please tell him I called."

He planned on marrying her and not telling me, continuing on with me as always, keeping the status quo as it had been with Jewel. But Jewel was gone, and it was insane of him to expect me to get used to a new wife. She was older than I and not much to look at, but in the end he married her and they adopted three children.

That was three years ago. He still calls me and always sounds miserable. I hope he is. As for Jewel, she hooked up with the father of her child; they bought a sailboat with the intention of sailing the world.

Iowa Was Never Like This

▼

Jane Smiley

I could have paid better attention to the signs. For example, I could have noticed that, both the first time around and the second time around, my husband Steve wooed me by detailing his exploits with other women, then flattering me by comparison—of all these women (dozens! hundreds!), I was the ultimate. Nevertheless, when he told me there was another woman, and that she was our dental hygienist, I at first didn't believe him, because not two weeks before telling me, he had remarked, with a straight face, that, should I ever find myself in a vegetative state, he would keep me, and even cherish me, in the living room of our house, so that he could personally fulfill my every unconscious need. But this is only context. He left me for the other woman; it was a shock; I vowed never to get into another other woman situation again.

I was forty-seven. I was living in California, no longer

in Iowa, and when I began to look round for male companionship, it turned out that there was some. In fact, it seemed like you couldn't move without stumbling over male companionship. Hardly trying, I found two physicists, a builder, and a veterinarian. I thought that at last I was in that enviable position that I had never been in as a girl, the position of being able to choose. Of course, each one (52, 55, 56, and 61) was possessed of both history and idiosyncrasy. The sixty-one-year-old introduced me to his favorite idea: "A wife, a mistress, and a little bit on the side." As I got to know him, I realized that I was intended to be the bit on the side. So, no go there. The fifty-six-year-old was earnest and attentive, but when I tried to explain to him what a metaphor was and how words in poems could mean more than one thing at the same time, he couldn't grasp the idea. I said, "What do you think about, then?" When he said "Usually equations," I knew he wasn't the one, either. I gave a dinner party and invited several friends, along with the veterinarian and the builder. Afterward, the friends and I discussed the party. The veterinarian, we realized, had talked only to the men, though he kept an eye on me and the other women, perhaps to gauge our response. The builder, we decided, not only talked only to the women, he possibly hadn't known that men were present. I thought, and no doubt said, "He's the one for me."

His name is Jack. He is the subject of this essay.

By this time I was forty-eight, almost forty-nine. Jack was fifty-five, almost fifty-six. I felt, instinctively, that I didn't have much time, and my instinct was confirmed on Jack's fifty-sixth birthday when he read me the card he received from his eighty-eight-year-old father: "Dear son, today you are fifty-six. Soon you will be seventy. Love, Dad." So I made up my mind to woo Jack by whatever means necessary. It was, in fact, a godsend that my house was falling apart. He repaired plumbing and wiring. He patched the roof and put windows in the barn. He fixed the whirlpool bath. The horses chewed the fencing and he replaced the boards. (He said, "That horse wouldn't leave me alone. He kept putting his nose in my tool bucket and then watching me pound nails." I said, "He likes you. He wouldn't go near Steve.") Also in my favor was the fact that he loved to eat and I was a good cook. Artichoke bisque. Risotto. Braised chicken with rosemary and mustard. Homemade French baguettes. He was a sensualist and I massaged his feet and his shoulders. No one knew we were dating because we didn't leave my house in four months. He would come over about eight-thirty and leave about ten-thirty.

But we didn't make love, because there was another woman.

The other woman pre-existed me. She and Jack had dated for about a year, and the relationship had been officially over for about a year. She was involved with two other men by the time I came along, an acupuncturist and the owner of an upscale antique shop. The acupuncturist was involved with several other women and wouldn't commit to N. The antique dealer had a shadowy past and his age was unknown, but he was willing to commit to N.

N. herself had several "bits on the side," one of whom drove a Rolls-Royce and was ready to leave his wife for her. Iowa had never been like this. Every so often I would ask Jack to describe N. She was, he said, "A sex goddess." In the meantime, my second husband, who was named Bill, decided to move to California to spend more time with our daughter. He rented an apartment in our village. I got on well with him and helped him move in. A few weeks later, I was sitting at a stop sign, trying to turn onto our main road. Steve passed through the intersection, traveling west, then Bill passed through the intersection traveling west, then Jack passed through the intersection traveling east. I thought, "Pay attention, this will never happen again." And it never did. Bill had a beautiful girlfriend back in Iowa who was still tangentially involved with her first husband.

After some hesitation, Bill started dating two women in California, a painter and a masseuse, but then he went back to visit an old friend and a woman at a party confessed to him that she had loved him her whole adult life, so he decided to commit himself to her. They are married now.

I continued to massage Jack's shoulders and inquire about N. She was ten years younger than I was, still in her thirties, and a potent force. I did things like try to ride my horse and try to write books. She did things like pose for artistic photographs exploring the nature of the erotic. She seemed to have extra powers. When she touched him, he would find himself shaking so uncontrollably that he would rise off the massage table and fall to the floor. I had never seen this, but I could imagine it only too well. All I had was a whirlpool bath and a good recipe for pork stew with fennel.

The other person Jack worked for was his former wife, who had left him for another man. Some years subsequent to their split, he had followed her to California for the sake of the children, and now she was living with the other man in the big house, and Jack was living nearby in the guesthouse, and helping them remodel their property for sale. When he came over in the evenings, I found myself consoling him and advising him not only about N. but also about his former wife, with whom he often disagreed, not about love or the children, but about building techniques. Truly, our circumstances were beyond California and practically to Scandinavia in many ways. At this point, no one we knew was actually married.

We went out to dinner with N. and the acupuncturist. He was heavy-set and hadn't cut his beard in a decade or more. His facial expressions were hard to understand because of the excess of hair, and he also didn't converse so much as he pronounced on things in a judicious tone of voice. She was dressed in a manner that would allow her to disrobe in less than a minute. Her necklace dangled right into her cleavage. The two of them were adamant vegetarians. How she could prefer this galoot to Jack I could not possibly imagine, but I could tell from Jack's manner that he accepted without question the idea that the two of them had some invisible quality that set them apart from second-level mortals such as ourselves. I don't remember what we ate.

The acupuncturist broke up with N. Jack spent several days consoling her, then came over and told me all about it. I then turned to Bill for consolation, but, as so often in the past, he wasn't interested in consoling me as much as he was in developing theories that justified the sense of social outrage our village induced in him. This was part of the reason we had divorced, after all. At last, Jack came over. The crisis was weathered. I clearly remember sitting up close to him at my kitchen island, drinking an evening cup of cinnamon tea, and him saying, "So she said to me, 'It's just you and me now,' and I said, 'You, me, and Jane.'" He smiled warmly. I was flattered. This was the first indication that I had reached parity with N.

In order to negotiate my new other woman situation, I lived by two principles that I still actually think are good ones. The first one is, Is the relationship you are actually in (as opposed to what you wish it were) better than nothing? Because those are your only real choices—this or nothing. Jack was kind, interesting, affectionate, a good conversationalist, and very funny, not to mention (or overlook) sexy and handsome. While he often talked about N., he did not actually seem preoccupied with her most of the time. When he was paying attention to me, he was actually paying attention. At least provisionally, sharing him with the sex goddess was better than not seeing him at all. The second principle was one I espoused to him: "You're fifty-six years old. You deserve to do what you want." Fifty-six years old seemed old to me at the time. If he couldn't do what he wanted by that age, when would he be able to?

But of course, there was the antique dealer. He was attentive. And, as N. pointed out, he had a boat. Within a couple of weeks, he got promoted to first position with her. The four of us entered into an uneasy double-dating relationship that occasionally involved Jack counseling the antique dealer how not to offend N. and yet manage her volatility. Personally, I found her degree of volatility unique to my experience and neither comprehensible nor respectable, but the two men seemed mesmerized by it. Most of the double dates ended in tears—not mine. I practiced appearing serene by comparison, which wasn't difficult but was sometimes simply a Zen exercise in solitary self-discipline. If I had an ace in the hole, it was that I wasn't much trouble. If there was a problem with my ace in the hole, it was that it was entirely possible, given Jack's marital and sexual past, that he might not recognize a woman who was no trouble as female. Every woman he had ever known sounded like trouble to me.

As the only specimen of "sex goddess" I had ever met, I found N. intriguing, but it was pretty clear that we were not going to be actual friends. Left alone, we had nothing to converse about; our tastes were entirely different; we had no common friends except Jack and, it appeared, no common interests of any kind, including boats. And in fact, a few years later, when the husband who had left me for our dental hygienist was on hiatus from that relationship, I set him up with N., just to test out her sex goddess identity with the most experienced philanderer I knew. He said he wasn't impressed. When I brought her out to meet my horses, though, the dominant male was fascinated by her, and wanted to touch her necklaces, her buttons, and her watch with his lips. When she took off her sweater and turned around to lay it on the grass, he actually tried to take hold of the back of her thong, which showed above the waistband of her jeans. This was the only independent assessment of her powers that I ever got.

The drama of N. and the antique dealer continued through the winter while, step by step, Jack and I approached and then achieved a sexual relationship. He seemed to be spending more time with me and less time with her. I lived by another principle during this period—Don't ask, don't tell—and I have to say it worked. Every so often, he would remark that she was a lot of effort. I introduced the phrase "high maintenance." He accepted it. In April, we went on our last double date, to a Rolling Stones concert. Everyone there was old, including us, including Mick and Keith. There was some kind of tantrum at the Rolling Stones concert that I can't remember, but I do remember that we all remarked on the fact that N. was only five years old when "Satisfaction" hit the charts. For once, this seemed a fault rather than a virtue.

A few days later, we left for Kaua'i, taking advantage of a week in someone's vacation home that I had purchased at a school fund-raiser. Subsequently, we agreed that what with the breakfasts I cooked, the fourteen hours every day in bed, the beaches, the waterfalls, the flowers, the laughter, the fresh fruit, and the scenery, this week in Kaua'i constituted the honeymoon for the marriage we still have not contracted. Shortly after we got back, N. and the antique dealer decided to go to Hawai'i, too. They went to the Big Island. While taking an arduous drive over the volcanic center of the island, arguing and in a state of some fear, they decided to get married, which you can do in Hawai'i on the spur of the moment, just as in Nevada. When they came home and told us this, Jack and I were both dumbfounded, but they assured us that they had gotten married solely because marriage was so unimportant that it wouldn't affect their relationship at all. And then, I have to say, the bearded acupuncturist returned from his sojourn to the Andes, or Tuscany, or the Lascaux caves, or whatever it was. He indicated that, yes, he wanted her back. Turmoil ensued. But by this time, the cost of maintenance had come to seem a trifle high to Jack, something like a twenty or twenty-five percent tax that he was less and less willing to pay. Comfort and, I believe, my true conviction that he had a right to do what he wanted, gave him the pleasure of not having to do everything he wanted.

We got domestic. Women who were trouble came to seem strange to him while I, a woman who was no trouble, came to seem feminine. There have been no other women since. Maybe we are too old for that. But what I think it is really, is that we got to be real friends, in addition to being really in love, and one of the features of our friendship was the difference in our relationships to N., relationships that we talked about openly, without defensiveness or, eventually, anxiety. He was honest; I was accepting; she was a force of nature.

Now, once in a while, she says that she wishes she had seen Jack's virtues when she had the chance, but my opinion is that she was too young to see them, and too certain of her powers.

ONCE UPON A TIME IT TOOK THREE

▼

Binnie Kirshenbaum

*There reigned abundantly the filthie sin of lechery and fornication,
with abominable adulteries, speciallie in the king.*

—RAPHAEL HOLINSHED
Chronicles of England, Scotland, and Ireland (1577)

It was a fairy tale of a wedding when, in 1981, Prince
Charles of the House of Windsor married Lady Diana
Spencer. The train on the bride's pearl-encrusted gown
was twenty-five feet long. Her shoes were also decorated
with pearls. She wore a diamond tiara. The newly wed-
ded couple rode through the streets of London in a horse-
drawn glass carriage. A fairy tale of a wedding and a fairy
tale of a marriage and, like many fairy tales, this marriage
was rooted in the Middle Ages; that is to say, it was a marriage of the nobility with a clearly defined purpose.

True, I have no idea what was in Charles's heart or
head when he proposed marriage to Diana (assuming he
proposed and not an emissary). Maybe he did love her,
but likely greater than any love was the pressure on him
to get married already and produce an heir to the throne.
Unlike the fairy tale, the prince could not marry just any

woman he fancied. There are guidelines, rules of order, lineage to consider. Diana fit the bill. Blue of blood, beautiful, graceful, a virgin (go find one of those in 1981), and fertile. In no short order, she bore two sons. An heir and a spare.

When not terribly long thereafter it was discovered, or rather publicly exposed, that Prince Charles had not given up his love affair with red-blooded and married Camilla Parker-Bowles (who was not a suitable wife for the no-longer-so-young prince), the public reaction, and especially the public reaction on our side of the Atlantic, was one of outrage, disdain, disgust, and the like. But why did anyone, including Princess Diana, think that this Prince of Wales would be any different from any other Prince of Wales, or, for that matter, any king, duke, or baron before him?

The nobility, the ruling class, the powerful have, since time immemorial (or thereabouts), arranged marriage for their children with clear agendum in mind: to forge political and military alliances, to increase the size of a kingdom, to stave off war, to fill the coffers, and, of course, to produce heirs whose bloodlines were all in the family. Often, the bride and groom were children; sometimes they didn't even speak the same language, but so what? This was marriage and marriage was business. If all went according to plan, sons were born, pocketbooks bulged, and war was averted. If all did not go according to plan, the marriage was dissolved and a new one was arranged. The dissolution of marriage got a bit trickier to pull off when, in the sixth century, the Church forbade divorce, but there was a lot of back-and-forth on the issue and more loopholes than fabric until well into the Middle Ages. But divorce, like marriage, bore no connection to either falling in love or falling out of it. A man took a new wife when it was politically or financially expedient.

The stakes might not have been quite so grand as with the nobility, but for similar reasons all marriages, until relatively recently in the grand scheme of Western Civilization, were arranged. For each strata of society, marriage was a purely pragmatic affair, an economic and domestic arrangement set up with a clear intent, a determined division of labor, and the pooling of assets necessary to survival. You got married to keep house and to have children. If you were lucky, your parents chose for you a husband who didn't beat you or a wife who was very fertile and very strong. It was fortunate for the man if his wife did not smell too terrible and fortunate for the woman if her husband was not fifty-six years old to her twelve. And if you were exceptionally blessed, you and your spouse came to care for each other, maybe even to love each other. Not romantically love each other or ardently love each other, but you might develop an affectionate love, a tender and caring love. As a component of marriage, passion and romance were frowned upon. Marriage was a rational affair; there was order to marriage. Rules and laws and honor. Nothing goopy.

Marriage was antithetical to Romantic Love. Marriage was rational. Love, as we all know, can run amok and make a mess of things. Even the language of love: lovesick, crazy for, losing our heads, spring fever, and the like all imply a kind of insanity or illness. To lose your head and throw caution to the wind was not conducive to married life upon which your very survival relied. Father knew best and it was best to let your father pick you a good bride or groom, with the same good judgment he'd use to pick a fine cow.

With the dismantling of the feudal system, cities and towns began to swell with population and commerce and opportunities of all kinds. Young people left the manor and flocked to where they could earn their own wages, which liberated them from their parents' stronghold on their futures. Young women could amass their own dowries and young men could establish their own households. Away from their families, they could choose their own husbands and wives. And so they did, but even then they did not marry for love. It was the custom to choose a partner who was just that: a partner. A man looked for a woman with, in addition to her domestic skills, a keen business sense, a wife who could assist him in his trade. A helpmeet. A woman needed a man who was able to provide a roof overhead and food on the table. Alone, a woman was faced with either a life in the convent or life as a courtesan (which at various points in the Dark and Middle Ages were not very different ways of life). It made no sense to marry a man simply because you got weak in the knees when he looked your way. You had to marry someone who would help keep you from starving to death.

And what then? Set up in his sensible marriage, his

belly full, now a young man's fancy (and a young woman's too) could turn to love. It might seem ironic to us that it took a solid and successful marriage to pave the way for romantic love, for passion, for adoration, and devotion for someone not your wife or husband, to flourish.

When the Roman philosopher Seneca warned that it was impure to love your wife as you loved your mistress(es), it wasn't the mistress who was to be denied the love. It was loving your wife that was frowned upon. To satisfy the need of that other part of human nature—the part that is passionate and lustful, the part that is romantic and sentimental, the part of ourselves over which we have about as much control as did Tatiana when falling in love with Bottom, the Ass in Shakespeare's *A Midsummer Night's Dream*—there was a tacit understanding: For love, for passion, and in many cases for intellectual companionship as part and parcel to love, men had mistresses. Women, although more covertly, had paramours, as championed by Eleanor of Aquitaine and Marie de Champagne. Courtly Love required a husband, a wife, and the man in love with the husband's wife. Our whole code of chivalry is predicated on adultery.

Ovid made no distinction between what we would call romantic love and erotic love, but early into the Middle Ages this conceit of Romantic Love developed its own set of rules that ran parallel to the rules of marriage. Blossomed into full and fragrant flower, Romantic Love was not only the inspiration for art—particularly in poetry and the songs of the troubadours—but Romantic Love, the pursuit of the beloved, became an art form unto itself. In the latter part of the twelfth century, back when priests and friars, as well as all the popes, did not resist the temptations of the flesh, a monk by the pen name of Andreas Cappellanus wrote a slightly tongue-in-cheek how-to book called *The Art of Courtly Love*. This book was hardly the only one of its kind at that time; Courtly Love was as popular of a sport as jousting. *The Art of Courtly Love* was largely a series of possible dialogues between The Man (the suitor) and The Woman (the beloved, who is never his wife). These dialogues were intended to instruct young men on how to win the hearts, minds, bodies, and souls of the women they desired. Contained within these dialogues are echoes of Seneca's dicta that there cannot be, there must not be, love between husband and wife. Now the word *love* had come to mean Romantic Love, which, despite an early and not surprisingly failed attempt at purity, did not exclude lust, but it no longer was entirely synonymous with lust, as it had been.

One reason, according to Cappellanus, why husband and wife cannot love each other is that love, in order to pulsate and thump like the heartbeat, must be kept secret. Marriage cannot be kept a secret. It is the secrecy of illicit love, that clandestine element, that fans the flames of passion. The intrigue is exciting. There is no intrigue in marriage. Moreover, the good monk illuminates, "another reason why husband and wife cannot love each other and that is the very substance of love, without which true love cannot exist—I mean jealousy—is in such case [marriage] frowned upon and they should avoid it like the pestilence;

but lovers should always welcome it."* This is, given the time and circumstances of love and marriage, a practical assessment. Love is hotheaded, passionate, and fickle. Marriage had to be stable and secure, and jealousy could muck that up.

Courtly Love was a neo-paganist ideal, despite—or in defiance of—the power of the Church in the Middle Ages. Curiously enough, this was a time when knights headed off to fight the Crusades for Christianity, but to inspire them to bravery they carried a talisman from their beloved, who was always a woman who was married to someone else. The legends of the great loves between the knights and their ladies—Guinevere and Lancelot and Tristan and Isolt—have it that ladies' husbands were the kings, whom we mustn't pity because surely they were getting plenty on the side too. So popular was this neo-paganism that even as the Crusades were coming to a close and the power of the Church was further reaching than ever before, Dante Alighieri was a married man when he fell hopelessly in love with his Beatrice. So much for the Sacrament of the Church. True love could exist only outside of the bonds of marriage, even for the author of *Paradiso*, *Purgatorio*, and *Inferno*.

The story of Abelard and Heloise (early twelfth century) is often thought to be the first citation of Romantic Love, as we perceive it: love that was nourished and grew, love

---

*Andreas Cappellanus, *The Art of Courtly Love*. Trans. John Jay Parry. New York: Columbia University Press, 1960, p. 100.

that was based on friendship and respect and the mutual love of learning. Love that did lead to marriage, but not until after Abelard had been castrated and sent his wife off to the convent, so it wasn't much of a marriage, but it was hot courtship. Yet Heloise did not want to marry Abelard, for fear that marriage would taint their love. Heloise was on to something: There is a direct correlation between the rise in the number of couples who marry for love and the rise in the rate of divorce.

The divorce rate is also higher in societies that place a higher taboo on adultery. A man whose wife doesn't much mind his having a mistress and neighbors who respond to the adultery with a shrug of the shoulders is a man who has no compelling reason to get divorced, to leave his wife and children. Family values, so to speak, were more rigidly adhered to when love outside of marriage was socially acceptable. Now we ask, demand, that the man (and woman) make a choice: Give up the mistress (or paramour) or get divorced, and we call it Family Values.

The love marriage—that is, love being the primary, if not sole, reason for marrying—evolved over time, gaining in popularity around the sixteenth century as surviving gave way to thriving, as, with the rise of the merchant class, life for many was not easy but not quite as arduous as it had been. There was some leisure time, and so young men and women were not only able to indulge in the luxury of choosing a spouse for themselves; they didn't necessarily have to select a wife who could pull a cart as well as a team of oxen or a husband who could spear a wild boar from sixty paces. They could now follow their hearts instead of their survival instinct.

The Reformation furthered the concept of the love marriage. Martin Luther preached that not only should husbands and wives have sex, but they should have sex for the pleasure of it. The Catholic Church's stand on sex was that it was for purposes of procreation only, a necessary evil, but Luther urged husbands to please their wives in bed, and to do it often. Not that Martin Luther was otherwise much of an emancipator. Along with this perquisite, the definition of adultery expanded. Now married men who had other women were considered adulterers too. Earlier, that particular commandment applied to women only, as the definition of adultery was a married woman having sex with someone other than her husband or an unmarried woman having sex with a married man. And Luther frowned upon young people marrying on their own volition. Parents, he believed, were still best equipped to make that decision for their children. But the notion of a fulfilling sex life between husband and wife, coupled with the idea that to be unfaithful was seriously sinful, took root. And during this time of the Reformation, along with King Henry VIII, came the Church of England, which was more lenient about divorce; a leniency that further encouraged the marriage based on love (because if the love soured, there was a way out). Therefore, the idea of marrying for love took strongest root in England. Moreover, the Reformationists held the belief that everything that happens, including falling in love, is ordained by God. The Puritans and the Separatists embraced this sanctification of love, and they brought the love marriage to America.

Consequently, we Americans have no history of Courtly Love and we have no nobility either, but we do have divorce. It's hardly that a philandering husband is unknown on our shores, but we do not shrug it off and look the other way, as is more the response on the other side of the Atlantic. (Although Starbucks isn't the only American trend making its way over; women and men there too seem to be adopting our sociosexual mores as well.) Nonetheless, when François Mitterrand, president of that bastion of Other Women known as France, died, we practically had apoplexy over the presence of his mistress and their "love child" at his funeral.

Yet for all our talk of Family Values, New York City's former mayor Rudolph Giuliani was not as reviled for having announced at a press conference that he was leaving his wife, the mother of his two young children, before he'd told her he was leaving, as was Bill Clinton when he owned up to having had sexual relations with that woman. This is not to condone Bill Clinton's behavior as much as to illustrate that divorce doesn't disrupt us the way a clandestine blow job does. Betrayal in our culture refers to straying (which implies coming back), rather than leaving (which implies no return). It is curious that our response to the former is far more harsh than to the latter. To divorce is to break a marriage vow and it breaks apart family. Why is it that we take the "forsaking all others" part of the pledge far more seriously than the "'til death do you part" part?

We ask a lot from our marriages, from our significant others, to be our everything . . . and forever. It's a tall order. We ask so much of them that they are bound, at some point or another, to disappoint us. But better to be disappointed, better to settle for what you've got, than to so much as consider that maybe there was something to be said for love on the side. But no. We are so entrenched in denying ourselves the pleasures of the seven deadly sins that for a man or woman to have his or her cake and eat it too is an outrage. Divorce is preferable to adultery. Divorce comes with loss and sacrifice, which is at least some form of punishment for the snake in the grass.

Despite the disappointments and divorces, the compromises made, the settling for something less than we'd hoped for, we hold dear our illusions, our fairy tales, which are the Disney version. In our fairy tales, when the prince falls in love with Snow White and Cinderella he, unlike a real prince, marries the little commoner. Neither one of them gets fat or watches too much television or is too tired at the end of the day or gets a blow job at the office. They live happily ever after.

So was it that Prince Charles of the House of Windsor did not live happily ever after with his princess that we could not accept? That his adultery resulted in our lost illusion? Was it his betrayal of our own dreams that angered us so?

One last question: Did anyone think that when he married Diana, Prince Charles had betrayed the woman he truly loved?

THE MISTRESS

▼

Dani Shapiro

Here, in no particular order, are some things Lenny told me: that he and his wife didn't sleep in the same bed; that they hadn't had a "real marriage" in years; that she was undergoing electroshock treatment in a clinic outside Philadelphia; that he had cancer and had to fly to Houston three days a week for chemotherapy; that his youngest daughter, aged three, had a rare form of childhood leukemia. That he could not get a divorce for all of the above reasons. That he was heartbroken that he could not leave his wife and marry me.

For a long time, I believed him. With every bone in my body, I trusted that Lenny Klein was telling me the truth. When we talked about it, his jaw would tighten and his big brown eyes would fill with tears. His voice would qua-ver with pent-up, complex feelings that I couldn't possibly begin to understand. Poor Lenny! I marveled that so many bad things could happen to one person, and I vowed to take care of him. Writing late at night in my extensive journals, I exhorted myself to be a real woman—one who could step up to the plate and be good to her man in his moment of crisis.

Years later—now—I hold Lenny's lies up to the light and examine my own reasons for believing what, in retrospect, seems preposterous. I reread my old journals and notice the way my girlish handwriting deteriorated into a scrawl as I wrote: *I have to be there for Lenny. He needs me, and he is going through so much. I don't know if I can handle it—but I have to be strong!* I try to remember that Lenny was a trial lawyer, that he built an international reputation based on his own pathology: that he lied with an almost evangelical conviction. He prided himself on being able to convince anyone of anything.

Paris, 1985. We are walking along the Boulevard St. Germain on a cloudless spring day. The rooftops of the Left Bank are creamy against a rare blue sky, and the air outside Café Flore smells of croissants and the acrid smoke of Gitanes, but I don't notice. Only now, as a grown woman, can I take in the rooftops of Paris, the extraordinary sky; I realize that in recalling this scene I am supplying it with a collage of my own more recent memories. In Paris, in 1985, I see only what is within one square foot of me, too busy feeling the complicated stew of sensations being with Lenny provokes. I am hungover, floating on a wave of last night's Puligny-Montrachet and a four-star dinner that wound up in the toilet of the Hôtel Ritz. Lenny's arm is around me, thick and proprietary, and it reminds me of the sex we had that morning, the way he pinned me to the bed and didn't let me move my arms until I came in spite of myself. In Paris, I am like an animal curled in a patch of sunlight, interested only in the beating of my own heart. Sex, wine, food, sleep. I am a physical being, living on the other side of a clear, thin membrane that separates me from anything to do with the world.

I have not read a newspaper or spoken to a soul other than Lenny for weeks now. I have been living the kind of unbelievable life people glide through in airport novels. We have been to London, Monte Carlo, the Côte d'Azur. I have played blackjack in private clubs with oil sheikhs who asked me to blow on their dice for good luck; I have driven a convertible around the hairpin turns of the Moyenne Corniche; I have eaten langoustine on a boat floating somewhere off the shores of Cap d'Antibes. I wear dark glasses and haute couture suits, a gold watch and a long, thick strand of pearls. I have no idea who I am.

Lenny steers us on to a narrow side street off the Boulevard St. Germain, and into a children's clothing store filled with the embroidered dresses my mother used to buy me as a child. He tells me he wants to buy a dress for his youngest daughter, the one with the rare form of leukemia. I help him look through racks of tiny dresses suitable for a three-year-old until we find one he deems perfect, a pale yellow silk smock with a Peter Pan collar. He holds it up to the sunlight and his eyes fill with tears. She'll never live to grow out of this dress, he whispers. My baby girl.

He has layered his lies one on top of the other until they have become opaque, an elaborate construction resembling reality. He is fond of quoting probably the only line he knows from Franz Kafka: *White is black and black is white,* he often says with a sigh. I never knew exactly what he meant by this, but it seemed to have a lot to do with my life at that time.

The lies had small beginnings. Lenny called me from a business trip and told me he was at Montreal airport, waiting to catch a flight to Calgary. I checked with the airline and found out that the flight would take approximately five hours. So when Lenny called an hour later to say he had landed in Calgary, I very calmly asked him where he really was.

"Calgary," he said. No, Lenny, really. He stuck to his story. In the time that I knew him he never, ever changed his story midstream. I hung up on him and called his family's house in Westchester. When the maid answered the phone, I asked to speak with Mr. Klein. And when he picked up the extension and I heard his rough, craggy *Hello?* I screamed so hard into his ear that he dropped the receiver.

He raced into the city. He let himself into my apartment and found me curled up in bed. He scooped me up and held me to his chest. His wife wasn't home, he told me. She was having shock treatment. And someone had to take care of his daughter. He hadn't wanted to tell me because he'd wanted to spare me, to protect me from the horror of his life. Surely I understood. *Ssshh, sweetheart,* he murmured into the top of my head as I wept, my face beet red like a little girl's. So *many people need me,* he said, *but I love you best of all.*

On our first date, Lenny Klein took me to the River Café, an expensive restaurant in Brooklyn with sweeping views of the Manhattan skyline. It was only when we were halfway there, driving downtown in Lenny's Rolls-Royce, that I realized I was on a date with my friend Jess's stepfather, and that we were not, as I thought, going to be planning a surprise party for her.

If only lives could be played out on movie screens; if only I could re-enter the precise moment when Lenny Klein picked me up for the first time and edit it, I would take the girl I was, that girl speeding along the East River, and shove her out of the car.

At the River Café, Lenny handed the maître d'hôtel a folded twenty-dollar bill. I had never seen anyone do this before. My father had always made reservations at restaurants and waited patiently at the bar if his table wasn't ready. Lenny and I were led to a window table with a candle flickering next to a small vase of pale pink roses. "Did you see that?" Lenny asked me once we were seated.

"See what?"

"The way you turned every head in the place. Don't tell me you don't know the effect you have."

The truth was that I hadn't noticed anyone looking at me, and I didn't quite believe Lenny.

"Do you know what I told Jess the first time I met you?" Lenny asked huskily, then continued, "I told her you were a golden girl. A perfect angel."

I flushed and looked down at my hands folded in my lap. I didn't know what to say. My last date had been with a senior named Adam, who brought along a six-pack of Coors and tried to feel me up outside my dorm door.

Lenny produced a pair of bifocals, then skimmed his finger down the wine list, frowning slightly.

A captain appeared at his side. "Can I be of service with the wine list, sir?"

"Do you have a 'fifty-eight Margaux?" Lenny asked. "I see the 'sixty-one, but—"

"I'm sorry, sir, we have only the 'sixty-one."

"Very well, then." Lenny leaned back in his seat and smirked at me. "This wine is older than you are," he said.

I knew what I needed to do. I knew I would be sunk if I didn't say something—and soon—about Jess, or about his wife. Not to speak up was to become Lenny's accomplice in whatever it was we were doing. But I felt paralyzed, and beneath that paralysis there was a frisson of excitement, an awareness of doing absolutely the wrong thing.

Lenny sniffed the cork and watched the wine being

decanted with all the fascination and reverence of watching a ballet. He swirled it around in his glass, took a sip, then gave a nod. "Pour just a bit for the young lady," he said. "It needs to breathe." When the captain left, Lenny lifted his glass slightly in my direction. "To beauty," he said.

I flushed more deeply and looked out of the window at a boat moving slowly up the East River. I had an inkling of how much this excited Lenny: young girl, old wine. For the first time in my life I felt my youth as power. (In years to come, Lenny would turn to me and ask how old I was: twenty, twenty-one, twenty-two, I would answer with a perverse sort of pride, knowing that my age acted as an aphrodisiac, knowing that his beautiful wife was, at forty, too old for him.)

I drank the wine and felt it slide smoothly down my throat, warming the tightness in my chest. I had no experience of the ritual of drinking fine wine. In New Jersey, growing up, I thought of red wine as the sweet Manischewitz we sipped out of thimble-sized silver goblets on Shabbos.

After the Muscovy duck, after the crème brûlée and cognac, Lenny leaned across the table and ran his finger down my nose in a gesture at once paternal and sexual. "I'll drive you home," he said with a wink.

Inside his car, I sat all the way over against the passenger door as he drove me back to Sarah Lawrence, my cheek hot against the cool window. I felt sick to my stomach. I thought of Jess, back at school. How would I ever tell her I had gone out on a date with her stepfather? Would she ever forgive me?

Lenny fiddled with the dial of the radio until he found a jazz station. A throaty trombone filled the quiet between us. Then, on a long straight stretch of road, he reached down, slowly and deliberately moved my long skirt up my thigh, and squeezed my knee. I knew I should tell him that I couldn't ever see him again, but somehow it already seemed too late.

Two years have passed, and something has gone wrong, terribly wrong, with my life. I don't, in fact, think of my life as "my life" but rather as a series of random events that have no logical connection. I am no longer a student. I dropped out of Sarah Lawrence after my junior year, supposedly to pursue acting. And I'm actually doing a pretty good imitation of an actress. You might even say that I'm playing the part. But I'm doing an even better imitation of a mistress. Lenny has been busy buying me things. I don't particularly want these things, but they seem to be what Lenny is offering in lieu of himself. So, quite suddenly, overnight really, I find myself driving a black Mercedes convertible. And just in case I might be mistaken for anything other than a kept woman, I wear a mink coat, a Cartier watch, a Bulgari necklace with an ancient coin at its center. The Mercedes is a step down from the first car Lenny gave me, when we had been going out for a month: a leased Ferrari. I didn't know how to drive a stick shift, so the Ferrari was a bit of a problem. What I must have looked like! A twenty-year-old blonde dressed like Ivana Trump, stalled in traffic, grinding gears, trying to find the point on the clutch to hold that ridiculous car in place.

Lenny rented an apartment on a pretty little street in Greenwich Village, a furnished triplex with a garden, a fireplace, and a bedroom with a four-poster bed. He called it "our house," as if he didn't have another home with a whole family in it an hour north of the city; he kept half a dozen suits in the bedroom closet, and a brand-new silk robe hung behind the bathroom door. There was an entire floor we didn't use: a large, airy children's nursery.

My parents knew that something was up. They knew I was going out with somebody, but they had no idea who. I was drifting away from them and they were letting me go. One night I invited them over for dinner. I pushed all traces of Lenny out of sight. But of course there were clues: a glossy brochure for Italian yachts; a humidor in the center of the coffee table; a man's Burberry overcoat on a hook near the front door. I cooked up a storm and the place was filled with homey smells: garlic, basil, coriander. It was winter and snow was piled up on the sills. Spotlights in the backyard shone on the landscaped garden, the redwood table, the Adirondack-style chairs, and the huge terracotta pots of last spring's dead geraniums. I had my father's favorite music, Dvorak's Symphony for the New World, playing on the stereo system.

My parents rang the doorbell. They looked so solid standing on my front stoop, their cold, red noses poking out from above their mufflers. If nothing else, they looked like they belonged together. They were elegant and rangy, similarly proportioned. (Unlike Lenny and me. Lenny is thick as a linebacker, and I had become so delicate the wind could have picked me up and blown me away.) My mother strode into the brownstone as if it wasn't the weirdest thing in the world to be visiting her daughter in a lavish apartment with no name on the outside buzzer. My father trailed behind her warily, as if setting foot on another planet.

My mother entered the living room, flung her arms wide, and did an impromptu dance to Dvorak. "Tra-la-la, tra-la-la," she trilled.

My father and I hung back and watched, our faces crumpled into awkward smiles. We were used to it. In every family there is room for only one Sarah Bernhardt, and my mother had assumed that role. It didn't occur to me that she was frightened, that this was a lot for her to take in, her college drop-out daughter living in the lap of luxury. All I could see was her outsized self, twirling around my living room in her fur coat and boots.

I wanted a drink. I walked over to my mother and put a hand on her shoulder, and she spun to a halt. I took her coat and my father's and hung them above Lenny's raincoat by the front door. For the first time I noticed that there was a wreath made of twigs, a bit of Americana, on the wall near the kitchen, and I wondered if I could remove it quickly before my father saw it. Wreaths, under any circumstances, are as goyish as it gets. Which would be worse for my father? Imagining that I was with some powerful guy old enough to be my father? Or the possibility that the guy wasn't Jewish? I wished I could reassure him. Yes, Daddy. He's Jewish. Twenty-three years older than me, a pathological liar, married to a woman who knows nothing of me—and a Jew.

I poured two glasses of Chardonnay for my parents and a large vodka for myself. I figured that if the vodka was in a water glass they wouldn't know the difference, especially if I drank it like it was water. My drinking had taken on a new urgency in the past few months. It was no longer a question of desire but of need. I could not get through an evening like this without the armor of booze. I handed them their wine and directed them to the couch. On the coffee table, I had put out a plate of crudités and a bowl of olives.

"Quite a place," my mother said brightly, her gaze darting around the room at the white brick fireplace with its wrought-iron tools, the glass wall overlooking the garden, the soaring ceiling. My father stared at the fringe of the rug, glassy-eyed. He needed to be as numbed as I did to get through this night.

"Thanks," I murmured, as if she were paying me a compliment. I checked on dinner, using the opportunity to gulp some wine from the open bottle in the fridge. Vodka and white wine was a combination I knew worked for me. If I stuck with the formula, things shouldn't be too bad in the morning. It would only become a problem if I switched to red or had cognac after dinner. I had learned to color-code my booze: clear (vodka, white wine) and colored (scotch, cognac, red wine) weren't to be mixed. Especially if I wasn't eating. And I couldn't see myself eating.

I had prepared my signature dish. It was my signature because it was literally the only thing I knew how to cook. A recipe out of *The Silver Palate* cookbook, it was a chicken stew of sorts, with white wine, olives, prunes, and brown sugar. I was serving it with wild rice and a string bean casserole I had bought ready-made at Balducci's. For dessert, a *tarte tatin* from Patisserie Lanciani. I had run all over the West Village preparing for this evening, thinking that my parents would be impressed by my culinary efforts; so impressed that, by the end of dinner, patting their full stomachs, they'd swell with pride at their only daughter who was, after all, living such a gracious and well-appointed life.

"Can I help?"

My mother was standing in the doorway. How long had she been there? Had she seen me take the swig from the bottle of wine? I tried to think of explanations. Thirsty was the only word I could think of. But then I realized that she hadn't seen a thing.

"Actually, I think everything's under control," I said, carrying the casserole to the table, which I had set with linen placemats and napkins. In the center of the table there was a vase of drooping purple tulips. The silverware, the pots and pans, the linens were all courtesy of the owner of this sublet place, a woman who I might—if

I had been thinking of such things—have viewed as a cautionary tale. A blonde, whippet-thin, fiftyish real-estate broker, she had lines around her mouth that weren't from smiling. She occasionally stopped by to fix something in the garden or the basement, and when I got near her I could smell vodka and stale nicotine just beneath a cloud of L'Air du Temps.

The music had stopped by the time we all sat at the dining room table, but I didn't notice then. If I had, I would certainly have changed the tape, filled the air with something other than the tinny, lonely sound of our three forks scraping against plates. I pushed my chicken from one side of my plate to the other; my stomach clenched and growled in protest. I had allowed myself one glass of wine in front of my parents, using a crystal wineglass from the set Lenny had bought me as a house-warming gift. It was all I could do not to down it in a single gulp.

It seemed that my parents and I, after twenty-two years in each other's company, had run out of things to say. I already knew their views on the political situation in Israel, and we couldn't discuss my schoolwork—I was no longer in school. My father pressed a corner of his napkin to his lips and murmured something about the food being delicious. My mother agreed.

"My wonderful daughter," she said, shaking her head. "You've turned into such a little homemaker."

I looked at my parents across the table. Is that what they really thought? How could they just sit there? Some small piece of me wanted my father to fling me over his shoulder and carry me, kicking and screaming, to the car he had parked outside. I secretly wished that they would drive me home to Hillside, deposit me in my childhood bedroom, and feed me chicken soup and saltines. I wanted to start my life over again, but I didn't know how.

I was afraid that I was going to cry, so I walked into the kitchen and pulled the apple tart from its box, arranging it on a cake platter. What had I expected from this evening? I thought I wanted my parents to be proud of me, to see that I was living like an adult. But even I knew that this wasn't true. We were all playing a game here, pretending that this was a nice family moment: mother, father, and daughter eating an elegant meal.

I presented dessert with a flourish. The *tarte tatin*, along with fresh espresso from the brand-new espresso-maker. Finally, the conversation—if that is what you call the words we spread over the gaps—veered, like the tide, in the only direction it could.

"Can't you tell us," my mother asked, as I took one bite of the delicious, flaky, apple tart, then another, and another. I was ravenous, like a starving dog. I'd make myself throw up later. "Can't you tell us," my mother asked, "who he is?"

My father cleared his throat. "It's been so long, Dani, it seems we really ought to know...."

I kept shoveling pieces of apple and crust into my mouth. I could actually feel my stomach closing around each morsel of food. The directness of their curiosity made me panic. My parents had been strangely passive on the subject of my dropping out of college and taking up with a mystery man. Over the past year I had returned from trips to Europe bearing gifts for them: Charvet silk ties for my father, brightly printed Pucci scarves for my mother. These were gifts I couldn't possibly have afforded to buy on my meager income from the few television jobs I got. Who did they think paid for them? And why did they accept them? Part of me was screaming to tell them, to just get it over with. After all, they had met Lenny on Parents' Day, when he came to see Jess. They knew who he was. Had he, even for a moment, crossed their minds as a possibility?

His name was on the tip of my tongue. It would have been so easy. It's Lenny Klein, I could have said, then watched the chips fall. Would they have been horrified—or relieved? What could they possibly be imagining? I was woozy from the vodka, wine, and the two helpings of apple tart. Okay, I thought to myself. Just say it.

"Is it Teddy Kennedy?" my mother asked. She was joking. It must have been a joke. But I could see that she had really considered this. She looked at me. Did she want it to be him? An image of the bulbous-nosed, red-faced senator from Massachusetts flashed through my head. My mother was staring at me, wide-eyed, poised for an answer, and suddenly I couldn't seem to say anything at all.

Lenny was in the middle of litigating a famous case, and there was front-page coverage in the New York

Times and the *Wall Street Journal*. In these pieces he was referred to as *flamboyant* and *feisty*. One reporter likened him to a bulldog, and another referred to his fleet of Ferraris and his trademark raccoon coat. Some people might not have welcomed this kind of coverage, but Lenny loved it. Just in case I missed any articles or photographs, Lenny had a messenger drop off clips each evening with my doorman. He'd never taken a case he couldn't win and I guess he thought he could win me too, if only he were persistent enough.

After all, in the face of the most tangible proof that Lenny had been lying to me all these years, I remained with him. The simple facts about Lenny—who, what, when, where— had always been elusive to me, impossible to grasp as he slipped and slid his way around the truth like a snake in a river. *My little girl is dying,* he would say whenever I noticed the discrepancies in his stories, or *My children's mother is having electroshock therapy.* When I couldn't take my own confusion anymore (Was Lenny lying to me? Was I going crazy?), I decided to hire a detective to get to the bottom of it. By this time my parents knew all about me and Lenny, in theory; but it wasn't something we could talk about.

When I think back to my younger self riffling through the New York City Yellow Pages in search of a private investigator, I feel like I'm watching a movie about some-one else, a girl so clueless that she really didn't know that her desire to hire a detective was all the answer she needed. I chose a detective agency based on nothing more than its good address, in the East Sixties, a neighborhood filled with private schools and shrinks. Most other agencies listed were in the Times Square area, or the Bronx.

It was a cool, crystal-clear spring day. I rang the ground-floor buzzer of a brownstone. A burly middle-aged man in a sports coat and polyester pants opened the door and ushered me inside. He had a thick head of sandy hair and fleshy pockets beneath his eyes. He looked exactly like my idea of a detective. I even noticed a trench coat hanging on a rack that stood by the door. He pointed me toward a small office furnished with a big library desk and two wooden chairs. The desk was covered with papers and half-opened manila folders with the edges of photographs peeking out. An old-fashioned phone, the kind with the dial instead of push-buttons, sat on a pile of magazines.

"Mrs. Shapiro?"

"Ms.," I replied faintly.

He blinked. "I'm John Feeny," he said. "We spoke on the phone."

For this scene I had dressed as conservatively as I knew how, as if, again, I were playing a role: pants suit, heels, and the pearls Lenny gave me for my twenty-first birthday. My hair was pulled back into a ponytail, around which I had wrapped a silk scarf.

"What can I do for you?" Feeny asked, not unkindly.

"You said on the phone that you sometimes deal with . . . personal business," I said. "I have a sort of weird situation."

He leaned back and rested his head in his hands, smiling as if to assure me that no situation could possibly be too weird.

"Ms. Shapiro," he said. "I was a detective on the New York City police force for twenty-five years before I opened my own shop. And I've been at this here thing"—he waved his hand around the room—"for a decade. Whatever it is, I'm sure I can deal with it."

I suddenly became afraid. Lenny's face could sometimes bulge with rage, and I remembered a story he liked to tell about how he had once picked up a broken bottle from the street and slashed a would-be mugger's face. Lenny was sort of a public person. More public all the time. I wondered if I was about to get myself into a whole lot of trouble. But still, I didn't get up, thank Feeny for his time, and head for the door. I stumbled on.

"This isn't what you think," I said. "I'm in a relationship with a married man. And I want you to find out if my boyfriend is cheating on me with his wife."

At this, Feeny's eyebrows shot up. "Come again?"

"He claims his wife is in a mental hospital. He told me he hasn't been with her in years."

"And you think he might be lying," said Feeny. Did I see the laughter behind his eyes, or is my memory supplying it now, because I simply cannot imagine a middle-aged man listening to an earnest, overdressed twenty-two-year-old girl tell him that she thinks her boyfriend might still be sleeping with his wife?

"Yes," I said.

"What's your boyfriend's name?"

"I'm a bit nervous telling you that."

"Ms. Shapiro, if you don't tell me his name, I can't possibly help you. What, is he some kind of famous guy?"

"Well, sort of," I said.

We stared at each other for a moment. "His name is Leonard Klein, he's—"

"I know who he is," Feeny responded dryly. "The lawyer guy." I nodded, then sat there, my hands folded in my lap.

"So what do you want? You want him followed?"

"I don't know," I faltered.

"You want pictures? Video? Tape? You want his phone bugged?"

I actually began to get excited. After years of trying to figure Lenny out myself, here, finally, was someone who was going to do it for me.

"Everything," I answered giddily. "I want everything."

"It's going to cost you."

"How much?"

Feeny pulled a pocket calculator out from somewhere beneath the mess on his desk. "Where does Klein live?"

"Upper Westchester."

"So there'll be travel. You want us to stake out his house?"

"Yes."

"Okay." He peered at the calculator. "I'll need a retainer. And I'm going to have to put a few guys on this. So why don't we say five grand?"

I panicked. That was about the total I had saved of my

own money. Everything else was what Lenny had given me: jewelry, a car, clothes, even cash from time to time. He had got me a credit card by lying to the bank, telling them I worked for his law firm. I had steadily been making less and less over the last couple of years; even my parents figured that Lenny was supporting me.

"Fine," I said quickly.

I had no idea whether it was a fair price for what Feeny was going to do, or even how I'd survive once I paid him. But I needed to know the truth about Lenny as if my life depended on it.

"Where's Klein now?" Feeny asked as he took the check.

"In Europe," I answered, "on a business trip. He's due back tomorrow on the *Concorde* from Paris."

"Fine," he said. "We'll start there."

Two days later, Feeny called to tell me that the passenger list for the Air France *Concorde*—no easy score, he assured me—showed a Mr. and Mrs. Leonard Klein traveling together. And the guy he sent to Kennedy Airport had spotted Lenny and his wife at the baggage claim. The photos were being developed.

Many things had occurred to me, but not this. I hadn't imagined for a moment that Lenny might be in Europe with his wife. Before he left on this trip he had given me a hotel number, and an associate in his law firm answered the phone at the Ritz each time I called. (I later found out that Lenny made a practice of this: He would fly a Harvard or Columbia Law School graduate across the Atlantic, check him into a hotel room, and instruct him what to say if I called.) Lenny had often told me his European business trips were top secret: meetings with Margaret Thatcher at 10 Downing Street, encounters with Russian spies.

In tears, I called my mother.

I found out that Lenny was in Europe with his wife, I said.

"Oh, darling, I'm so sorry. Is there anything I can do?"

"I don't think so." A pause.

"Do you want me to call his wife?"

My mother and Mrs. Klein had met each other at a few school functions back when none of this could have struck anyone as a remote possibility.

"Yes," I said. "Call her."

"I'll do it right now," my mother said.

I sat by the phone and watched the minutes tick by. I pictured Lenny's wife answering the phone with a chirpy hello, and my mother's slow, steady explanation of why she was calling. I had set in motion a chain of events that was now unstoppable. More than twenty minutes passed before my mother called me back.

"Well, I did it," she said.

"You talked to her?" The world felt unreal, hallucinatory.

"Yes. She called me a liar. She told me that she has a happy marriage to a man who travels a lot. That he's on his way to California. And I said, 'No, he's on his way to see my daughter.'" My mother sounded proud of herself, immersed in the drama of the moment.

"How did she seem?" I asked.

"What do you mean?"

"Lenny's wife—was she angry?"

"No," my mother said slowly. "She just didn't believe me, Dani."

I spent the rest of that day in a state of awful excitement. Something was going to happen. And when Lenny showed up that evening at the apartment we were still sharing in the West Village, I was ready. He put down his bags and gave me a hug.

"How was Paris?" I asked.

"Exhausting," he said. "Nonstop meetings."

"Really."

He looked at me oddly, but we didn't have time to get into it. The phone rang. My mother had given Mrs. Klein the number at the apartment and suggested she find out for herself what her husband was up to.

Lenny picked up the phone on the kitchen wall. "Hello?"

I watched him, and for the first and only time in the years I knew him, he looked genuinely surprised. He didn't say a word. He just listened for a few minutes, then hung up the phone.

"That was my wife," he said.

I was silent.

"How did she get this number?"

I shrugged.

"I have to go."

"I'd imagine," I said faintly. My anger was giving me

the fuel that I needed to stay strong, at least for the moment.

When Lenny slammed out of the apartment, I was certain I would never see him again. I knew the truth now. It was staring me in the face, in the concrete form of flight lists and photos. And he knew that I knew. And besides, the whistle was blown. What could he possibly tell his wife?

This was it, I told myself. Absolutely, positively the end.

It wasn't the end. Lenny still called ten, twelve times a day. He left messages on my answering machine. *Hello.* His voice filled my bedroom. *Fox? Are you there?* Sometimes he didn't say a word. He would stay on the line for as long as five minutes, just breathing. I know he thought he could get to me again. But I was trying harder than I ever had before to stay away from him. Sometimes he would call in the middle of the night and wake me out of a deep sleep; my hand would reach reflexively for the phone. But I always managed to stop myself before it was too late.

Eventually, he did get to me again. And for the next year that we were together—three days here, four days there—my life became unrecognizable to me. I idly wondered what it would take to get me to leave him. I wondered about this over bottles of chilled white wine, or heavy glasses half-filled with scotch.

I was still wondering about it when I went to stay for a while at a health spa in California. The phone rang in my room one day. There had been a car crash on a snowy highway. My mother had eighty broken bones. My father was in a coma. They were lying in a hospital 3,000 miles away, and suddenly—in ways I could not have imagined seconds earlier—nothing else mattered. As I packed my bags, I remembered my mother twirling—dancing to Dvorak—through the doors of Lenny's brownstone, and the glassy look in my father's eyes. I prayed that my father wouldn't die disappointed in me, and I knew then what I had to do.

THE LOVES OF HIS LIFE

▼

Katharine Weber

When Angela came to dinner that first time, I had been warned in advance to say nothing about her missing right arm. I was told not to stare, not to ask questions. She lost her arm in The Blitz, my mother told me just before the guests arrived. I was six, and did not know what The Blitz was, but it sounded bad if you could lose your arm in it. We were living in London for most of that year (instead of our ordinary suburban New York house) because my father was producing a movie of *Macbeth*, which was being filmed at Pinewood Studios. Judith Anderson was in the film, and she came to dinner that same night, but she had two arms and she didn't make much of an impression on me, though I remember the sound of her laugh when the adults were still at the dinner table and I had been tucked into my bed upstairs. She had one of those laughs that has nothing at all to do with whether or not the person laughing thinks something is funny.

We were in a little rented house in Knightsbridge, on Rutland Place. It was 1961. Buskers, most of them tattered veterans of "the war," I was told, came around our corner playing the accordion or the violin, and I would give them some of the dime-like sixpences and the thick thrupenny bits from my hoard. 240 pennies in a Pound Sterling! Once, when I was sorting out all my money on the sitting room carpet, my father told me some men said "thrupenny bits" to mean something dirty about women, but I didn't know what he had in mind and my mother told him to be quiet. One of the buskers had a monkey on a leash. The monkey wore a little red outfit with a matching hat. He took my pennies, put them in a little change purse he wore around his neck, and bowed in thanks.

Milk in glass pints was delivered every morning in front of the gate at the end of our brick walkway by a horse-drawn milk wagon. The horse wore a straw hat with holes for his ears. There was thick yellow cream clogging the necks of these bottles, cream that my older brother would devour greedily at the breakfast table, which suited me fine, as I hated it. Once I tried to bring in the milk by myself, but when I opened the gate, being too short to reach over for the bottles, one of the bottles got knocked over, and broke. I was ashamed. Neighborhood cats lapped up the creamy puddle and then I was glad the bottle had broken, proud that I had provided this feast for them.

Judith Anderson had also laughed her pretend laugh

at my puppet show after dinner, before I was put to bed while all the grown-ups and my brother stayed at the table. We had a folding wooden puppet theater with a red curtain on a string. It was not too hard to carry it into the dining room and set it up to give everyone a show, once I had finished eating. I knew they thought I was very cute and industrious. I pretended to ignore them but was pleased as I carried in the puppets and set up for my show.

All through dinner I had not said a word, but I had watched Angela as she ate, using her only hand. She had long red nails, and pretty rings that sparkled. Someone must have helped her with her nail polish. She was fascinating. She was beautiful. She wore dark red lipstick. Her hair was tucked in a sleek chignon. The lipstick she could do on her own, but not the hair. She wore a dark green knit suit, and a matching little hat she never took off. She seemed unaware that she was missing a body part. She cut her meat with her knife in an inexplicably deft gesture and then picked up her fork, as if this were the most natural way to eat, as if everyone ate this way. Why had my mother served roast beef, of all things?

My mother, an indifferent cook at best, wore no makeup and cared little about her looks. She walked heavily, as if it pained her. She was mostly preoccupied with my problematic brother. She had none of the exciting features that made Angela almost intoxicatingly vivid to me. The man who had brought Angela, someone named Bill who made government-funded commercials to be shown in movie theaters about things like why eating tuna fish was a good idea, didn't offer to help her cut her meat the way my father sometimes helped me cut mine. I tried to eat dinner using just my left hand, not switching the fork back into my right hand after cutting my bites, but just keeping it in my left hand. I didn't want anyone to see that I was imitating her, but nobody noticed. After that night, I always kept my fork in my left hand when I ate. I still eat that way.

Because we lived not too far from an elegant toy store, Hamleys on Regent Street, forays into this nirvana were a regular feature of our days, usually on our way back from walking in a nearby park. My mother, a lover of toys and toy stores, had bought us, over a series of those visits, quite a collection of articulated wooden marionettes made by Pelham Puppets. We had Hansel, Gretel, the woodcutter, the witch, and two elegantly dressed nameless females, whom we called Blondie and Brownie. There was also a prince, a cat, a dog, and a horse. These puppets were a little more than a foot high and had twelve strings each. Manipulating them was tricky. Their arms and legs were strung loosely on the strings like wooden beads. They were not knotted at the ends, and so the elements that made up the arms and legs could be slid up the strings, completely out of view of the audience, if armlessness and leglessness should happen to be part of the narrative arc in your puppet show.

My after-dinner puppet show that particular night featured a great deal of armlessness and leglessness. Most of the action seemed to consist of the woodcutter attacking the fair maidens to chop off their arms and legs with the ax he held permanently at the ready in his right hand. The ax had its own string and I had become quite adept at developing the swinging motion to convey realistic chopping. Up the strings all the arms and legs would go as I whisked the fair maidens offstage for a moment, and then the torsos of the victims would return to dangle helplessly while bemoaning their sad fate until Hansel and the prince would come to the rescue, vanquishing the woodcutter and somehow miraculously restoring the missing limbs of the fair maidens in the process. The restoration was very satisfying, because all that was involved was letting drop all the arm and leg parts, which I held in a bunch gathered up at the top of the strings where the strings were knotted through the two-piece wooden frame. The reconstituted arms and legs would slide down the strings and re-attach to the bodies in an instant, but then the woodcutter would break free and start hacking away at his victims again, and the whole scenario, complete with flyaway arms and legs, would be enacted once more.

I have no idea how long my puppet show went on, how many cycles of arms and legs being chopped off and then miraculously returned were played out before the curtain fell. It might have been five minutes and it might have been a half hour of this repetitive drama. I do recall very attentive silence on the part of my audience, except for that piercing, fake movie-star laugh. After the applause, I took my bows and I kissed all the grown-ups good night, one by one, around the table, and Angela smiled at me and put her hand on my shoulder as she leaned down to kiss me good night. She wore strong perfume that lingered on me pleasantly as I lay in my bed listening to the sounds of the dinner party. It was still daylight and I wasn't sleepy. I was not reprimanded in any way, and my puppet show was never spoken of again after that night. I was in my twenties when it dawned on me what I had done.

Angela met my father for the first time that night, she revealed to me, on the one occasion I ever saw her again, a couple of years after my father's death in 1983. He had stopped speaking to me on my twenty-fourth birthday, in 1979, for reasons that grow only more inexplicable over time and had to do with his unfaithfulness to my mother, his declarations to me that he wanted to leave her at last, and my taking him at his word. Angela's romance with my father began soon after that, she said, and was possibly already underway when my mother, brother, and I flew back to the U.S. a few months later and my father remained in London for another six months. I didn't ask her for clarification about the timing. Because by now I knew that Angela was one of the loves of my father's life. He had spent years with her, though my parents never divorced and my mother never acknowledged my father's infidelities, or even his prolonged and mysterious absences. Acquaintances could have been under the impression that my father had stepped out for a sandwich during stretches of many months in my childhood when, in fact, I knew that my mother had no clear idea about what country my father might be visiting, let alone when he might come back to us.

My husband and I met with Angela for lunch at the Dorchester to discuss the complexities of my father's tangled estate. An important document had been witnessed by her in a hotel room in Cannes. She had been in partnership with him on some completed production guarantee bonds. She might be able to resolve some of the mysteries surrounding his estate. (But she never did.) She had possession of the Mercedes he kept in London. She may have had possession of his fancy Patek Philippe watch as well, but it seemed tasteless to ask, though my husband had seen it on my father's bedside table just hours before his death, in Wellington Hospital in London. Angela was with my father when he died.

When we learned that my father was suddenly and unexpectedly dying of brain tumors in London, my husband offered to make a quick trip with my forlorn and helpless mother to see him. She agreed, thrilled by his offer, as she would never have even considered making the trip on her own. They stayed just two nights in London. The hospital staff had been perplexed when Nick showed up with my mother to make the eleventh-hour deathbed visit. Until the arrival of this odd American woman they had never seen before, they had thought the devoted Angela was Mrs. Sidney Kaufman. (I didn't go because I had just given birth to our younger daughter, and didn't want to leave her, and didn't want to take her and leave behind our older daughter, then twenty months old, and

I didn't see a reasonable way to make this trip, under the circumstances, with the two of them.) On her last moment ever with her husband of thirty-eight years—at which point he had already slipped into a coma, though he had been aphasically conversational the afternoon before—my mother did not know what my husband knew because of what he had glimpsed as they walked down the hallway towards my father's private room: that an elegant, turbaned, one-armed woman had slid gracefully into the bathroom and locked the door just as they arrived at his bedside. My father died just hours later, while my husband and mother were flying back to New York.

In the weeks and months after his death, I joked about Angela to my friends. In response to my descriptions of the byzantine issues of his mysteriously modest estate, when a friend asked, "So did Angela get her hands on all the missing money?" my reply was a witty "*Hand*." The one-armed woman was preposterous, like a marvelous Iris Murdoch invention. But meeting her for lunch two years later, that afternoon at the Dorchester, the truth was that I had always felt admiration for her, I had always felt a peculiar kind of fondness for her and a kinship with her, this odd, one-armed woman who never married, was a working barrister most of her life, and who, strangely enough, also owned a florist shop. She had loved my father and he had loved her. She looked like a somewhat faded Duchess of Windsor that day at the Dorchester, same sleek chignon, another elegant suit, the red nails, the rings, the perfect lipstick. There was something almost unbearably touching when the maître d' whispered to the waiter that we should be shown to "Mr. Kaufman's table." This had been her life. At the end of lunch, the awkward financial inquiries at an end, my husband suddenly asked her if she could solve another Sidney Kaufman mystery. Warily, she agreed to try. Why, Nick asked, given that he was always the very last person to board a flight, was my father always the last to get off a plane? To meet a Sidney Kaufman flight was to wait and wait and worry that he was not on the flight at all, until finally he would emerge, long after all the other passengers had passed by. She thought a moment and then her face lit up. "I imagine," she said, a smile playing on her lips, "that he would have been delayed gathering up all the little soaps from all the lavatories on the plane."

When I was eight, I couldn't go to sleep at night. My father was away, who knew where or for how long. I would roam around the house, spying on my mother while she read to my brother, spying on my mother while she read alone in her bed, spying on my mother after she turned out her light and listened to the radio in the dark, the tinny sound of a Yankees game from the West Coast or the sonorous voice of Long John Nebel the only sound left on which to eavesdrop. I went upstairs to the third floor and roamed around the attic like a secret agent, rummaging for clues, searching for the truth. I discovered a hatbox filled with letters. There were dozens of letters tied in a bundle that my father had written to a woman named Rosamund.

There was a matching bundle of letters Rosamund had written to him. I read them like a novel, night after night. They had begun their romance in 1939, or at least that was the date of the first saved letter, when each was married to someone else, though her husband was coincidentally also named Sidney, and the letters continued through the time period when my father met and married my mother, and Rosamund met and married someone named Paul, through the year we lived in London. Her letters were addressed to him there, on Rutland Place. The last letter, from Sidney to Rosamund, was dated 1962, just the year previous to the one in which I found this collected correspondence. His letters to her were tender and ornate in their declarations of love, of passion. He quoted poetry I didn't recognize. This was a side of my father I didn't know at all, and perhaps my mother didn't know it either. There were dozens of receipts for hotel rooms for Mr. and Mrs. Sidney Kaufman, from 1939 to 1962. His last letter to Rosamund was about how desolate he felt alone at the motel after she left, and how he backed his car over a little black kitten and killed it, and then how he sat sobbing on the ground beside the dead kitten. The letter was smeared in places, as if he had cried while writing to her in his familiar, angular fountain-penned hand. All of her letters were typed, on onionskin paper. I read and reread these letters night after night, carefully putting each letter back into its proper envelope, preserving their order, putting them back precisely where I found them each night.

One day, I was watching television and was surprised

by a screenplay credit for Rosamund's husband, Sidney. I asked my mother as casually as I could, at dinner that night, if she had ever heard of him, saying I had seen his name on the titles of an old movie on television that afternoon. My mother replied yes, he was an old friend of Daddy's, and you know Rosamund, that book editor who shares Daddy's office? She used to be married to that guy, a long time ago. "But he was a sonofabitch," my mother added.

When I was twelve, I met Rosamund. My father took me to his office and introduced me to her there, saying, awkwardly, "This is Rosamund. She could have been your mother." She was very pretty, very tailored and crisp. She wore a beautiful striped blouse tucked into a wide leather belt cinched around her waist. Her straight skirt was wrinkled from sitting at her desk. My mother did not own clothing like this. When she dressed up it was in her Girl Scout Leader uniform. Rosamund chatted with me, looking into my eyes in a knowing way. What she didn't know was how much I had already come to admire her, how I had studied her letters to my father and soaked up all their wit and originality, all her elegant turns of phrase, her wandery associative style; how I had begun to imitate her physical writing traits as well, her use of dashes to break up long sentences, her habit of double spacing to begin new paragraphs, which she did without indenting. We three had lunch together. She asked me about my writing and listened seriously to my shy, hesitant answers. I began to meet her for lunch, just the two of us, every few months. This went on for years. She was an editor of nonfiction. She told me I ought to write about my maternal grandmother, who wrote Broadway show tunes and was known for her romance with George Gershwin. We talked about novels. I didn't keep our lunches secret from my mother, but I didn't feature them, either. My mother was as oblivious to my carrying on with Rosamund as she had been to my father's involvement with her, it seemed. He and I had a bond, our secret Rosamund connection.

When my father stopped speaking to me, Rosamund stopped calling me. By then they no longer shared an office, and I don't think she saw him very often. Her husband Paul was elderly and ailing. She had retired from her publishing job. The day after his death, when my father's obituary appeared in the *New York Times*, Rosamund called the house. My mother answered the phone. "Uh-huh," she said, and then I saw her scowl, and then she said, "The hell with you," and she hung up the phone. "What was that?" I asked her. "Rosamund." "What did she say?" "Do you really want to know?" Yes, I really did. "She said, 'Kathy must feel so guilty,'" my mother said. I was sorry I had asked.

I have no idea if Rosamund is still alive today. It's possible. She would be in her nineties. I have changed her name in writing about her. I hope she lived long enough to see my novels in print. (The first one featured an adulterous man missing all his toes who hides under a table in a restaurant, an unconscious gesture in the direction of Angela's performance at my father's deathbed that I didn't appreciate until the novel had been in print for a year.) I want her to have read them, I suppose, out of a mixed desire to show her up and to show them off and to show her that nothing I got from her was wasted on me. Angela died some ten years ago. I had half hoped she would leave my daughters something in her estate, perhaps in that way making up for the riches my father appropriated from my mother that may well have gone her way, or perhaps it was all stashed in a forever unattainable Swiss bank account—every family needs its myth of the lost fortune, doesn't it?—but all there was, in the end, was a brief note penned by her personal secretary to say she had died. I didn't really need anything more from her than what I had already been given.

INVITE THE BITCH TO DINNER

▼

Ellen Sussman

When I married my husband in 1979, love and lust were a package deal, two for one, lifelong warranty, come on down. I was twenty-four. I loved my man and spent a lot of time in bed with my man.

Then two years later, I went to a writers' colony and met A.G., a guy who made my heart race. My skin changed temperature as if embers of a fire glowed just below the surface. And though all we did was talk—and talk and talk—late into the night, sitting on the deck of the cabin we shared with a group of other writers in the Sierra Nevada Mountains, I had never felt so much need to touch someone in my life. I imagined his mouth on mine, his hands wrapped around me, his clothes splitting at the seams and flying across the room. Meanwhile we discussed our novels, our jobs, the state of publishing, our wonderful spouses, and, no, we never ever discussed our desire for each other. I imagine he lusted for me in the same way—otherwise he would have gone to bed hours before, and the next night he would have found some other writer to talk to. But we spent a week in lust, talking endlessly, and, finally, on the last night at the conference, he gave me a back massage. It was exquisite torture, that hour we spent with his hands roaming the terrain of my back, kneading my muscles as if he wanted to push his way through them and into my body, then lightly brushing his fingers over my skin, electrifying me. He left when he was done and I never slept that night.

The next day, when I returned to hearth and home in Los Angeles, I was wildly confused. I loved my husband—how could I still desire another man? I was that young. And being that young and that naïve, I decided to share this shocking conundrum with my beloved.

We sat in the living room of our small Brentwood apartment where the walls were so thin we could hear the arguments of the young couple next door. We weren't like them—we were happy, in love, and reasonable enough to talk about my first married crush while sharing a bottle of Chardonnay.

"We didn't *do* anything," I told my husband. I didn't mention the back massage—even Pollyanna knew that we had crossed some boundary there, even though the man's hands never strayed. "But I don't understand," I went on. "I mean, I *love* you. I didn't think that could happen again. I felt like I was sixteen."

I didn't say I *loved* feeling sixteen again.

"Good," my husband said, and from behind the living room wall someone shouted, *Fuck you!*

"Good?"

"I've been meaning to tell you—"

A door slammed. Next door.

"What?" I asked.

"There's a summer associate at the law firm. Nancy. We've been working together all summer. I don't know, I like her. I have a crush on her. Or something. We haven't *done* anything—she doesn't even know—"

"Invite the bitch to dinner," I said.

Before I introduce Nancy—before I let her take over my essay the way she took over my life that summer—I think I'll keep her to the sidelines for another moment. I'd like to poke my finger into the hot belly of my own crush first. A.G. was good-looking, though not knock-out handsome. I can barely remember his face now. I remember that he was thin and dark and spoke in a low voice. In fact, it's his voice I remember, its quiet serious-ness, its hint of shyness. I remember his novel, too, a long slow novel about a baseball player in the throes of October madness. I'm not a baseball fan, but I loved his book and read it as if reading love notes written expressly for me. I don't think there was a sex scene in the book, but I would have taken the ballplayer to bed in a second.

A.G. seduced me with his writing. He charmed me with his dreams of writing more novels, wonderful nov-els, novels that simmered like hot buttered rum inside of him. He was a journalist by day, a Writer by night. I lusted for his words.

My husband was a lawyer. He dressed like a lawyer in suits and starched collars, spoke like a lawyer with convoluted sentences that needed to be decoded, thought like a lawyer with a maddening sense of logic. And though I loved him, I lusted for my writer, my twin, my soul mate.

I remember an evening, early on in our marriage, when my husband called me at home, where I was writing, and told me to come to the law firm in Beverly Hills for an impromptu party the senior partner was throwing. I tossed on a summer dress and dashed over. When he met me at the elevator he scanned my body, his face twisted into a scowl.

"You're wearing that?" he asked.

"What's wrong with it?" I asked. It was an Indian print dress, with a low neckline and a short hem. I might have been wearing a bra, but I'm not sure.

"Nothing," he said quickly. We were still newlyweds, after all.

Now my husband lusted after a lawyer, a woman who styled her hair instead of finger-combing it, a woman who wore power suits instead of bedspreads, a woman who spoke of contracts instead of epiphanies.

Enter Nancy.

He invited the Bitch for dinner. I wanted to know who she was, what she was. I wanted to hate her in person. It didn't matter that I had just cheated in my heart;

I wouldn't allow my husband to lust after anyone but me. My husband was willing to invite her to our apartment the following weekend. He had nothing to hide, he promised. Except a little inner turmoil, nothing that we couldn't put to rest over salmon burgers.

Nancy was a man's woman. She wasn't pin-up beautiful, but she had a look. And he was looking. She was thin and tall; I was curvy and short. She had a husky voice as if she'd spent years drinking whiskey with her Wonder Bread. She threw her head back when she laughed—I had only seen women do that in the movies, older women, daring women. Not twenty-three-year-old girl-women.

She paid no attention to me. Everyone paid attention to me! I was exotic, I was a writer, I was wild. She didn't care about any of that. She talked about the securities case she and my husband were working on and he leaned toward her across the table, his lips wet, his eyes moist. She didn't flirt; she wasn't coy or girlish. She was intense and brilliant and I wanted to murder her.

But I sat demurely at the dinner table in our small apartment, and even the feuding couple next door were curiously quiet. Everyone was so damn well behaved I wanted to scream. But no need for theatrics—my husband wasn't cheating; he was just longing for this brainy beauty while I sulked in my ice cream sundae.

I remember an earthquake in L.A. that summer—one that made me run from my room to the doorway that overlooked the kidney-shaped swimming pool in the courtyard below. The water in the pool splashed out, though no swimmer stirred the surface. The man next door appeared and, clinging to his own door frame, stared below. "Crazy," he said. "Can't trust a fucking thing in this town."

I always trusted the calm surface of my husband's love. Now, shaking it up at the core, was Earthquake Nancy.

"You were quiet this evening," my husband said when Nancy left and he finally looked at me.

"Not much to say," I lied.

"I wonder if she's sleeping with any of the other summer associates," my husband said, almost to himself, while we headed toward the bedroom.

"She has a boyfriend," I said. "She said that during dinner."

"I know," he said, and he drifted dreamily toward bed.

Nancy left Los Angeles at the end of the summer and returned to law school in San Francisco. I never saw A.G. again; my husband never saw the Bitch again. My husband and I survived Our Summer of Lust. I wonder now, years later, if we should have paid closer attention to that odd confluence of crushes. We were already looking for someone else, someone who understood us, someone who shared our passion. We never would have said to each other: I need more. I need something else. We wouldn't even say it to ourselves. But while the couple in the apartment next door threw plates and screamed obscenities at each other, my husband and I lay quietly in bed, imagining someone else's body hovering above.

Being a competitive soul, I don't want Nancy to be the only Other Woman in my story. I wanted a chance at what I thought would be the glamour role.

Ten years later, my husband and I moved to Paris. I taught writing classes to adults and my classes were filled with interesting Anglophones from many countries, with a wide range of stories to tell. One student, Marcel, came from Switzerland and was a few years younger than I. He was married, multilingual, and handsome. He wrote brilliant stories about men who fell in love with Other Women.

Marcel invited me to visit the Eiffel Tower one day. Oddly, I had never been. Tourists visit the Tower, not ex-pats. But he knew the effect of the Tower, the dizzying view from the top, the romance of Paris spread like a sepia-toned photograph at our feet. We zipped up in the elevator, stepped out onto our perch, gazed below, then gazed at each other. He took me in his arms and kissed me. I was so surprised that I kissed him back. Then he confessed his love for me.

I have to admit I did not love Marcel. Not even close. But it was Paris. We spent an afternoon walking the streets of the Left Bank, kissing in doorways, pretending we were a Robert Doisneau photograph come to life. And then I went home and called him and said that our kissing affair was over.

The next day he told his wife.

"You told your wife what?" I asked.

"That I love you."

"But I don't love you," I insisted.

"It doesn't matter," he said. "I have fallen in love with another woman. My wife must know."

I was horrified. I was a marriage-breaker, all because of the damn Eiffel Tower. I pleaded with Marcel to forget me, to love his wife, to drop my classes, to write wonderful literature under someone else's tutelage.

Years passed. I've lost touch with Marcel, though someone told me that he won a literature prize in Switzerland and that his winning story was about an affair in Paris. I imagine it must have been fiction or based on another affair or conjured out of a kiss.

Because of Marcel, I discovered that it wasn't much fun to be an Other Woman. There were consequences that I couldn't imagine while locking lips on the Seine. Someone else loved Marcel, loved her marriage, loved the passion that had once been directed her way. I had been playing *amante* for a day while someone else was home, waiting for her man.

Jump forward many years.

My marriage ended. Soon after, I fell in love with a man who was more of what we like to call a soul mate. He's an artist (furniture designer and builder), a renegade, a man without a suit in his closet. (Well, he gave them away when he stopped practicing law, but you get the picture.) When I first visited him at his ranch in Washington State, he woke me in the middle of the night to watch the Perseid Showers paint the sky. For almost a year he wrote me e-mails that read like poetry. And though his legally trained mind is logical and sharp, he loves the twists and turns of my jagged brain.

A month after we met, he arranged a dinner in San Francisco so I could meet some of his closest friends. He's a man who loves women—many of his best friends are women. He couldn't wait for me to meet his dearest law school friend, his cohort in late-night card games and bourbon fests, someone he swore I would just adore.

Nancy.

My old nemesis sashayed into the restaurant and back into my life.

I recognized her the moment I saw her. She was attractive and self-assured and threw her arms around my man.

"Remember me?" I asked.

"No."

"Remember my ex-husband?" I asked, offering his name.

"No."

And with that, she went back to hugging Neal.

I watched her closely during that dinner at Lulu's. She had aged a bit—but that streak of gray looked exotic in her thick black mane. She was married, had two children and still practiced law, still charmed the table (not me! never me!) with tales of her brilliant career. And her whiskey laugh had deepened—I noticed that when she threw back her head, all of the men in the restaurant turned her way.

This time it's different, I told myself, quieting the murderous whispers in my heart. I'm more mature. I know that we're complicated sexual beings and that a hot hussy—I mean an attractive old friend—won't shake my swimming pool.

"But you must remember our dinner in L.A.," I insisted when our entrées were served and I saw Nancy lean over to spear an asparagus from Neal's plate.

"No," she said flatly. She shrugged. "Long time ago."

I pressed on, but Nancy didn't remember much about her summer in L.A., and certainly didn't share my husband's infatuation. He hadn't even registered on her radar. I should have been pleased—instead, I was furious. Didn't we matter? The answer was clear: I didn't matter then and I didn't matter now. She sat next to my new beau and spent the evening talking about the wonderful memories they'd shared. At the end of the evening, I said something to her about the amazing coincidence.

"What coincidence?" she asked, having forgotten me again.

"Isn't she terrific?" Neal asked me later.

I growled.

"I love you," he told me. He did. He took me to bed. He wasn't lusting after Nancy; he was lusting after me.

Still.

I hate it every time he tells me that Nancy called. I

hate it when they have lunch together, which isn't that often, but more than I'd like—which would be never. When he returns home from their lunch, he could at least mention that she's aging or skinny or difficult, but maybe that's asking too much.

Nancy, my Other Woman, doesn't threaten me. But she haunts me. She reminds me that she'll never go away. That one can't take love—or lust—for granted. We don't need to sleep with other people to jeopardize a marriage. One friend of mine lost her husband when he found another woman who became his confidante. She and I have spent years speculating that they must have been sleeping together, but maybe they never needed the bed. She lost him when he gave something else away—his attention, his secrets.

I invited the Bitch for dinner. We were having a dinner party that included many of Neal's old law school friends, a gang I otherwise adore. At one point in the evening, Nancy sat next to me at our outdoor table, and as the candles flickered in the late night breeze and someone filled my wineglass and someone turned up the African music, we talked about life and love and literature. She's okay, I thought. Besides, I've got the guy.

The next morning, the phone rang. I picked up and Nancy said hi. In a quick moment I thought: She's called to thank me. To say how much she enjoyed talking to me. To tell me that it was nice to connect with each other instead of with my husbands.

"Can I talk to Neal?" she asked.

"He's not home."

"Oh. Well, I just wanted to tell him how great it was to see him last night."

I might have forgotten to give my husband the message.

CASSANDRA

▼

Caroline Leavitt

It's 1970, a hot day in Pittsburgh, and Emma, my sister-in-law and best friend, is taking ten minutes just to enter the doorway of the psychiatric hospital.

She pushes in the revolving door, paralyzed with terror. Everyone looks lost here, even the doctors. There's no sense of anyone getting well, and when she gets on the elevator, she doesn't know why, but she opens her purse and swipes on lipstick.

The doors open on the fourth floor, and she takes a step forward. People in street clothes are wandering around. A nurse whisks past, arguing with a doctor. Someone is bellowing, "Ger-on-imo! Ger-on-i-mo!" and Emma looks toward the sound.

Dan, her husband, is in the far corner. He's naked and he's pounding on his chest, staring straight ahead. He was a brilliant doctor and this is his third psychotic break, his third round of shock treatment and meds, and when he gets out again, he'll be so loving to Emma, so funny and smart, that you'd never know anything was ever wrong with him. Not until the whole cycle begins again.

"Ger-on-i-mo!" he shouts, gorilla-banging his chest. Emma, heart thudding, edges quietly back into the elevator and stabs the ground-floor button. And then, as she always does, she rushes outside, gets in her car, calls me, and tells me everything.

I loved Emma the moment I met her, which wasn't long after I married her brother, Tom, five years earlier. She's small and beautiful, a talented painter, and everything about her—her willingness to reveal herself, her sense of fun, her staunch support—are things I'm beginning to miss in Tom. All of us live in Pittsburgh now and the main topic of conversation bonding Emma and me together is the sudden sorry state of our marriages.

The day before Dan was committed to the hospital, we were all at Emma's. She was whisking shrimp into hot oil, so it snapped and sizzled in the wok. Tom was sitting sullenly in the living room and when I saw him get his jacket, I grabbed his elbow. "Don't do this tonight," I say.

"Can't I even go get cigarettes without you thinking I'm having an affair?"

I try to touch him and he sidesteps. "You're always going someplace that doesn't include me," I say quietly.

He zips his jacket. "Stop," he says. "Just stop."

"That jerk," Emma says when she discovers he's gone.

She knows the story, because I confide everything in her, and even though he's her brother, she's annoyed and on my side. She scatters salt over the shrimp. Dan is snapping his head back and forth like a metronome. He mutters something and taps his fingers against the wall. Emma turns toward him. "Dan?" she says. "Honey?"

He leans toward her and says something I can't hear.

He walks unsteadily out of the room and Emma looks at me, defeated, and puts the spatula down. "He's getting sick again. He's hearing voices and he's talking to them. I'm going to have to call the doctor," she says. Wearily, she shuts off the flame. The shrimp have burned in the pan. Dinner is ruined.

Dan is in the hospital for a month and he has a new doctor named Alex Coter, who is tall and in his sixties, with a shock of black hair. He gives Emma a list of foods Dan can't eat because they'll interfere with his meds, and he wants to start talk therapy as soon as Dan is out. "It would be a good idea for you to come in, too," he tells her. "It will help you help Dan."

"Fuck," Emma says, but she makes an appointment.

Marriage sucks for both of us these days, but it draws us closer. Both our husbands are somehow gone, Dan locked up and Tom on mysterious business trips and late nights at the office, and when I call him, no one answers. One night, when Tom doesn't come home, I call Emma at three in the morning. "Cab over," she orders. "Don't be there when he gets back," and I do. In the morning, the phone rings at six and Emma grabs it from me. "Oh, *now* you want her," Emma says. "Now that she's the one who's gone." Emma winks at me before handing me the phone.

It's winter and Emma has been seeing Alex for three months and she's dressing for her appointment, sliding on a new black dress, taking time with her makeup. "He's so nice," she tells me.

Of course it's transference. Alex tells her that at every session when she blurts, "I love you." But so what? Feeling love is glorious. She's energized and painting and she has a glow. He's warm and reassuring and he always pulls the conversation back to why she shouldn't consider Dan's illness her fault. "I think," he tells her, when she starts crying, "you should come see me three times a week now." She looks up at him. She hides her delight. I'm jealous but I tell myself, think of what Emma's going through. Think of what it would be like to be married to someone like Dan.

It doesn't really help.

She knows it's ridiculous on some level that she's turned into a cliché, the woman who loves her shrink and hopes he loves her back. She spends one afternoon trailing Alex, and when she sees him with a woman, she goes to his office and demands to know who the other woman is. "You know that's not your business," he tells her, and then he says, "Her name is Nita and she's a nurse, and that's all you need to know." That night, Emma sprays the sheets with perfume. She lights candles and puts on her prettiest nightgown and takes Dan to bed. He can't perform. The meds suppress desire and make sex impossible, but still there's cuddling, there's closeness. He sits up, knocking one of the candles to the floor so it catches the edge of the curtain. "Oh!" Emma cries and stamps the flames out, and the room smells like smoke and defeat. "It's all right," she says, and though she curls up beside him in bed, he doesn't answer. He stares at the wall and rolls away from her.

One day, the first thing Emma says when she walks into Alex's office is, "I love you." She's wearing jeans and a silk shirt, and she can't look at him without feeling nearly hysterical with desire. Alex stands up and comes toward her and she shuts her eyes. "Don't give me a fucking Kleenex," she says.

He licks her eyelids. He kisses her hair, her mouth, her neck. He pulls her on the floor and every time he touches her, she feels a jolt of heat. She stops crying. He pulls her panties down and opens his pants, and then he's inside of her, one hand gently over her mouth so she won't call out and disturb the patient just outside the door.

It's over in ten minutes, and he helps her up. He buttons her blouse tenderly. And he kisses her mouth. Neither of them speak. When she leaves his office, her panties are damp and her mouth is swollen, and she thinks the sex was terrible but she feels this beam of joy inside of her, flashing like a go signal.

She calls me and tells me and I hold my breath in wonder. "I did everything for Dan for years," she tells me. "He can't sleep with me anymore. He won't ever get better. I haven't left him. Don't I deserve happiness?"

"Of course you do," I tell her. I want to come over, I want to hear more of the details, but she tells me she wants to paint. She's fired with creativity. "I'm going to do his portrait," she says.

I'm alone in my house. I don't want to write my novel, though my deadline is looming. I don't want to do anything, and then I go outside and there is Tom, standing on our porch, and his face is terrible. "I want a divorce," he says.

I shove him, so that he stumbles. "Are you seeing someone?" I scream.

"That was animal consciousness," he says coolly and then he leaves me there, weeping.

"He's seeing someone, I know it," I tell Emma when I call her crying, and as soon as I tell her I'm calling a lawyer and I'm moving to New York, she cries, too.

"Don't go," she pleads. "This is your home. Stay here. He's a jerk but I know he loves you. He'd tell me if he was seeing someone—I'm his sister, for God's sake."

It changes. All of it. I go to the lawyer's and pack and call my friends in Manhattan, who tell me to come stay with them until I find a place. I call my agent, who tells me I can work in the office until I find something better. "Was there someone else? Do you know?" I ask my friends in Pittsburgh. I even call all of Tom's friends. No one knows anything.

Emma is wonderful through it. She stays with me, she takes me to lunches I can only pick at, and she tells me how she and Alex are always together now. "Things have a way of working out," she says, and what she means is that Dan just got out of the hospital and told her he wants to try living on his own, that it doesn't mean he doesn't love her, he's just not sure he can handle the relationship. He has no idea that Emma and Alex are a couple, and in fact, he still goes to Alex for therapy.

"Alex says as soon as Dan is stable and working again, I should think about divorce. I should marry him."

I grab her hands. "God, I'm so glad something is working out for one of us!"

"It will work out for you, too," she promises.

It doesn't, though. The day I leave for New York, Tom has been gone for two days. "He just can't bear to see you leave him," Emma tells me. She's at the house, helping me finish up, waiting for the cab to the airport. I know she's being nice, and I hug her. "I'm going to miss you," I say.

In New York, all I want to do is forget my past. I throw myself into my work and finish my novel. I find a shoe-box studio in Chelsea and I start seeing a man I fall in love with, a guy who wants to be with me all the time, who calls and comes over when he says he is going to. And every week I speak with Emma. "Dan has a girlfriend," she tells me. "A bank teller in a little bunny fur." She tells me Alex is practically living at her house, and when I ask, inevitably, if Tom had had a girlfriend, if he has one now, she sighs. "Absolutely not."

A week later, I'm getting ready to go out with my boy-friend when the phone rings. "Why can't you leave him alone?" a voice says. She says her name is Stella and she's been Tom's girlfriend for four years now. She tells me all the things I wanted—needed—to know. How she met Tom when he was buying a present for me, how they tumbled into love. And then she tells me how Emma joined them for dinner all the time, how she covered for Tom so I wouldn't know they were a couple. I couldn't breathe. "I have to go now," I say.

I pick up the phone again and call Emma. Her voice when she answers is breathy. "Fuck you, you lied!" I shout. "You covered for Tom! You knew he was seeing someone else and you never told me!"

She doesn't deny it. "He's my brother, you're my best friend. How could I choose whom to hurt?"

"Fuck you," I say again. And I hang up before she can explain. For weeks afterwards I let the machine take my calls and the second I hear her voice, I delete the message.

So what happens with Emma while I am living my new life, a single young woman in the big city with a busted marriage and an ex-best friend? Emma, of course, feels terrible. I am no longer in her life, but Alex is, until one day she goes to his office, impatient about getting married, and he's wearing a plain gold band. "Aren't you jumping the gun?" she teases, but he looks serious. "Emma," he says, slowly. "I married Nita, my nurse."

She jerks to her feet, her head pounding. All the colors drain from the room.

"Nothing has to change between us," he says, but she starts throwing things in his office, books, his framed diploma. She yanks open drawers, ready to scatter them, and it's then that she sees all the condoms, like balloons, just waiting for the next occasion.

She doesn't eat. She doesn't sleep. It's Tom who tells her Alex needs to be stopped, who finds her the high-powered lawyer, and it's the lawyer who finds out that she's not the first patient Alex has slept with. "There've been lots of other women," he tells her. "And they want to testify. But you need to use your full name now. You can't be Jane Doe."

Of course it makes the papers. Of course Dan, living in his little apartment, sees it. He gulps two hundred Seconals and never wakes up. His parents call Emma to tell her she's not welcome at his funeral. And the trial is about to start. Her lawyer calls me, and as soon as I hear her name my heart slams shut like a door. He asks, "Would you be willing to testify on her behalf?"

I think of how Emma lied to me about Tom. I wasn't just cheated on by Tom. Emma cheated me, as well. "I can't," I say, and Emma's story goes on without me.

*   *   *

It's three in the morning, and Emma's asleep when the phone rings. She struggles for the receiver. "Yeah?" she whispers.

"Cassandra," a voice hisses. "Cassandra—"

The phone goes dead. Emma knows who Cassandra is. The poor woman in the Greek myth punished by the gods by being forced always to tell the truth and never have anyone believe her. When the phone rings again, she yanks the plug out of the wall.

The calls don't stop. She buys a big dog, Jean-Luc, a standard poodle that she walks every day. One day, when he's been outside in her backyard, she calls him, and when he doesn't answer, she's frantic. She checks the neighborhood, and an hour later she finds him in some bushes, dead. Hysterical, she cradles him in her arms. She carries him, heavy, cold dog, all the way home, where she gently puts him in her car and drives to the vet and insists on an autopsy. The vet, when he comes out to talk to her, has a funny look on his face. "I'm sorry," he says. "He's been poisoned." And even though Emma can't prove it, she knows who did it.

Two days later, she is in a courtroom, staring straight ahead, one of six women sitting beside three lawyers in expensive suits. Tom is in the audience. She feels Alex in the room, but she doesn't look at him. She stares straight ahead day after day, and when the other women take the stand, she closes her eyes. When they call her, she's sweating, but her lawyers have practiced her and she knows what to say and how to say it and that day, when she goes home, she spikes a fever of 102 and throws up all night.

Alex is found guilty and she and the other women are awarded millions. He can't practice anymore. He's going to prison. Nita has left him. After the sentencing, Emma stands very straight and doesn't look at Alex, though she feels him watching her. When she walks out of the room, for a moment, she remembers the way he had touched her naked, but she keeps walking.

She gets an unlisted phone number, but it doesn't matter, because every time the phone rings, she still jumps. She buys a new dog, another poodle she calls Marcus, and she keeps him with her all the time. One day, he bounds away from her and races into the brush and she screams at him so harshly, he stops in his tracks. A young mother, walking with her daughter, pulls the girl closer. I'm sorry, Emma wants to scream. *I'm sorry, I'm sorry.*

The Greek gods always punished humans for pride. Alex gets a cancer so virulent, he's dead in months. The day she hears, Emma begins seeing a new shrink, a woman. "When there's a shrink involved, it's never the patient's fault," the new doctor says. Later, the shrink tells her that whenever she relates Emma's stories to the psychiatric students she teaches, the room gets very quiet.

One day, Emma notices colors again. Experimentally, she drives by the hospital where Dan spent so much time and, when she doesn't feel sick, she pulls over by the side of the road, the motor idling, her heart racing. Continuing to where Alex had his office is harder, but she feels like this is something she has to do, and when she gets there, it's boarded up. And then she drives to the bank and takes out some of the money and begins to spend it, and it's the first time she can without crying.

This story begins with Emma but it ends with me. It's late one night and someone I loved has died and I want everyone who ever hurt me to know that this may be terrible, but I had something special, I was loved. I'm angry and desperate and flooded with grief. I call Tom and he's surprisingly kind. "Whatever you need, I'm here," he says. I call Emma and, for weeks afterwards, I call her every night because she lets me rant on the phone and carry on and she doesn't ask me to listen to her life. Not yet. Not until I'm ready. And when I am, her story spills out and I'm stunned.

"Do you forgive me for not testifying?" I ask.

"Do you forgive me for not telling you the truth about Tom and his girlfriend?"

Neither of us needs to answer that.

"Will you call me again? Can I call you?" she asks.

I stop a moment. We each breathe into the phone.

No one's cheating or being cheated on. Not Emma with Alex, not Tom with Stella, not Emma with me or me with Emma. The past is past. The betrayals are over. The scabs have formed.

I hold the phone against my face. "I'll call you tomorrow," I say.

THE UTERINE BLUES: WHY SOME WOMEN CAN'T STOP FUCKING OVER THEIR SISTERS

▼

Connie May Fowler

The Other Woman (let's call her TOW) is as omniscient as air. She drinks with us, breaks bread with us, confides just about everything but *that* with us. She is our co-worker, our boss, our best friend, our mother, our sister, our daughter. She is, I believe, on some level, what every man desires and what many possess. She gets his non-exclusive dick, a little bit of his precious time, and his good moods. She doesn't wash his dirty underwear, take flak for his shirt collars not lying just the way he likes them, or listen to him complain endlessly about work. She could never claim to be an Xbox widow; there's no time for him to play Kill Switch when illicit pussy is in the room and the clock is ticking. If he has kids—and maybe even if he doesn't—he most likely wines, dines, and pampers her more often than he spoils his legit woman. After all, he has a full-blown life, complete with ups and downs, joys and sorrows, with the woman who washes his shorts. TOW isn't part of the complex construct of daily life, but rather an escape from responsibility and duty. She's a slit in reality's scrim, a two-hour vacation, a selfish or needy or weak man's fulfillment of fantasy and ego. And she is tragic. Yes, despite her abundance, her sheer numbers, her self-evident place in society, she is invisible, anonymous: the freakin' unknown dishonorable soldier of the heart.

I've dealt with TOW all my life, and I have to be honest, I really hate the bitch. My childhood memory vault is filled with episodes of my mother alternately weeping and cursing because Daddy had been gone for three days, holed up at TOW's house. One time he stayed with her for an entire month.

My runaway daddy always, eventually, retreated from his fantasyland TOW and returned home—a brave move given Mama's napalm temper. Whenever he walked through the front door, whether it was nightly, biweekly, monthly—we never knew—the ensuing shouting matches were spectacular. Mama was a dirty fighter with a mean mouth. Many nights, after running to my bedroom for cover while she screamed at him, I thought that if I was Daddy I'd have a girlfriend too. But when you're five, it's difficult to ponder which came first, the cheating or the bat-shit hollering.

When I was in my early twenties, I fell in with a man who behaved just like my father: charismatic, handsome, disloyal, and violent. Talk about old-home week. I found out about the cheating thanks to the universal spirit we call God who is, I believe, a thrice-jilted woman who watches over women who are all too likely to get caught up with philanderers, thanks to their childhood role models. The man—I'll call him Jerko—told me he was going to play poker with his sons. Of course I believed him. I always believed him. About a half an hour after he left the house, I headed to the grocery store and who do I pass? You got it. Jerko was pulling into a liquor store. I thought, What a nice surprise; I'll just stop and say hello. Oops. TOW—whom he'd been seeing for a few years, I later found out—was in the car with him, sucking more than his face.

I became my mother, wholly righteous, ablaze with fury. It did no good. He didn't break it off with her. For all I know, my hold-no-prisoners pain gave them a good laugh *and* fueled their passion. But that's okay; he wasn't true to her either. He was the kind of cheat who'd get a blow job in a public bathroom from someone he'd just met—the lonely waitress, the sodden barfly. He couldn't help himself. It was as if his entire skewed sense of self-worth was tied to his indiscriminate dick.

As for his TOWs? I want to say they were pathetic. But that's dishonest and unfair. In truth, they were just like me: They wanted to believe he was a good man, that he loved them, that they had a future with the asshole.

I finally found my ovaries and dumped Jerko, only to find myself plagued with a TOW of a different complexion. The Other Woman—the bitch, the liar, the cheat,

125

the no-good-keep-me-awake-and-crying-all-night cuntress—plagued my marriage before the *I do*'s had slipped our lips.

Initially, TOW was a no-emotional-ties kind of gal: a swinger. That's right. Sex R Us was the name of her shop—no hearts allowed. She enjoyed group and anonymous sex and could talk trash like a revved-up garbage disposal. She didn't care if he was engaged, married, widowed, or quadriplegic. She simply liked what his dick—all swollen and erect—looked like in those Polaroids I found one day while cleaning the apartment. They were stashed with the swinger newspapers (pre-Internet), other photos of him (taken in our bedroom), and her and her, and her, and her friends, and tawdry letters promising access to hidden, stinky places.

I discovered that swinger TOWs are legion. AIDS or no AIDS, from the fat pages of the tabloids he had stashed behind the bedroom bureau, it appeared that a lot of women were soliciting secret sex and they weren't discriminating about where it came from. Like their garden-variety sisters, they lived in the shadows, members of a secret society damned to living as if they were nothing more than half-muttered phrases. Except in the pages of the now defunct (I'm assuming they are defunct) monthly swinger tabloids and global Internet sites such as Adult Friend Finder, Swing Life Style, and even My Space, the swinger TOW has no cachet in polite society. Yet, eternally, her perfume wafts through our lives like an ominous wind ripe with forbidden fruit.

Crushed at the discovery of my fiancé's secret life, I begged him to stop. No, that's not wholly true. Actually, when I found the material I collapsed onto the terrazzo floor and curled into a fetal knot. He promised it was a misunderstanding and pledged to always be true. So I married him.

But something freaky happened. I believe his need for swinger TOWs morphed into an obsession with naked-model TOWs. I have to be fair here: this is my assumption. In his mind, the two might have been unrelated, but to my way of thinking, which I admit was shaded by fear and hurt, swinger TOW and naked-model TOW were loose threads—wild, errant little numbers—plucked from the same steel shawl.

The anguish the new type of TOW instilled (or did I instill it in myself?) pockmarked my heart long after my divorce papers began to stink with the musky scent of a single woman with too many dogs. Don't misunderstand me. I'm not accusing my ex of engaging in a long string of tawdry, meaningless affairs. I really don't know how he spent his spare time. What I do know is that he was devoted to the naked-model TOW. She eclipsed me. His devotion appeared consumptive, as if she were life itself. He spent hours alone with her, studying her naked form through his viewfinder. He touched her gently, lovingly, as he posed her. He gave her sweet directions in a voice he never used with me—it was a tender voice made kind and plump with awe. And after he was finished photographing her, he spent days in his darkroom, conjuring countless images of her naked body from a toxic stew of photo chemicals.

Me, I spent countless hours staring through windows, watching him watch his model. Without a doubt, when he looked through the camera's lens and studied her fair form, he did so with desire and longing and a sense of grace that were totally absent when he glanced at me.

I did all sorts of things to get his attention. I skinnied down to a size five. I cajoled editors at local newspapers to run stories about his nude portraiture and helped organize shows at galleries willing to risk censure and criticism about the content of the work. On the outside I was the supportive, proud, beaming wife. Inside, I was dying. It wasn't the fact that he had such intimate and emotionally rich relationships with his naked-model TOWs. What devastated me is that he and I did not have a connection that in any way approximated what he shared with them.

And they knew they were superior in his eyes. Other than for my dog sitter, an endearing flower child who looked at it as a groovy happening, and a young woman who was an admitted exhibitionist whose boyfriend was always present, the women treated me with the dismissive disdain of Cinderella's evil stepmother. When I finally faced the truth—I would never be his golden girl; he would always seek other women to fill that interior space—I experienced the same seismic shift as the wife who finally admits that her husband is never going to stop cheating.

You might argue that his obsession with naked-model TOWs was not, technically speaking, cheating. I would counter that an endless series of sexually and emotionally charged (platonic or not: I'll never know) affairs with women who—shutter click for shutter click—returned his intent gaze, giggly and nipply, feeling fully adored and perhaps even loved, is infidelity posing as art. He, after all, was making them immortal. Me? I was lucky to get a slap on the ass.

Yes, yes, I know: I have culpability here. The reasons I stayed too long in relationships riddled with varietal TOWs are gnarly yet predictable. Daddy issues. Mommy issues. Abandonment issues. Self-esteem issues. But I'm learning. I swear. Take, for instance, the journey I began after I left the aforementioned man. I call it my year of living dangerously.

I wasn't alone. My friend Laura, who is significantly younger but wiser in so many ways, joined me. We were in the same boat: newly single, newly lost, both of us in search of a man who would provide ballast in our lives. We set sail on Saturday nights and, believe me, we were sirens on that wide sea. We never brought men home; indeed, we never slept with a single one of them—we were looking for love, not sex—but boy oh boy did we learn a lot. Married men bobbed about in the singles scene like sneaker waves, leaving long trails of broken hearts in their wake. I asked one man who was hitting on both Laura and me what the problem was with his marriage.

"There is no problem," he said, his eyes shining bright with hearth-and-home enthusiasm. "I have the best wife on the planet. We've got a great marriage."

Then why was he in a bar trying to pick up women? Maybe he had a need for wild sex. "So, are things not hot enough for you in the bedroom?" I really wanted to understand this guy.

"No, things are great. I couldn't ask for anything more."

Then he invited us up to his hotel room where, he said, we could get naked, get in the hot tub, and let whatever happens next happen.

"But that would make us abettors. And you just said you love your wife, that you have a great marriage. How can you cheat on her?" I asked.

He swirled his drink, stared into it as if it would give him the answer. "It's not cheating."

"Then what do you call it?" Laura asked.

"A good time," he said.

Despite the choppiness of these high seas, Laura and I still held on to the naïve hope of discovering that indefinable groove we call love. After months of dodging creeps, I thought I found it.

I met Mr. X at a dance club. He was friends with the band and didn't seem like a player; he was there simply to listen to the music. We immediately hit it off. He was smart and witty and single, and had intriguing credentials: a former NBA player and a successful entrepreneur. His laughter sounded like ice cubes being tossed into fine crystal. He'd been in town only a few weeks and was involved in a business venture with several partners. He hadn't moved totally; he still kept an apartment up north, which, he told me, he would give up as soon as the business was fully established. Within a couple of weeks, I had fallen overboard; I really liked this guy. But my year of living dangerously had made me a much more watchful voyager. Why, I wondered, did he shuttle back and forth between his apartment up north and his place in Florida almost weekly? Business, he said. I bought it.

But the 3 A.M. phone calls that he would take outside on the porch and conduct with whispered urgency could not be business. I didn't care what he said. And when the Fourth of July rolled around and he once again had to go north on business, I was no longer able to ignore the signs. The phone conversation went something like this:

"You've got to go on a business trip on the Fourth of July?"

Silence.

"Hello?"

More silence.

My stomach lurched—truth hurts. "You're married, aren't you?"

He started laughing, those ice cubes clinking one by one, shattering my illusions. "How'd you know?" he asked.

I ended things right there and commenced to mourn for two days—just as if he were nothing more than a forty-eight-hour flu bug.

But he kept calling, trying to be charming and upbeat and claiming the divorce papers were imminent. I never responded to his divorce-talk, knowing it was a lie fueled by self-delusion and a brand of emptiness no woman could fill. The last time we spoke, he wanted to know if, when he retired in a few years, I would move with him to the Caribbean. He had a whole novel laid out as to what our life by the sea would look like. We would get old and gray together in Paradise. We would eat fresh fish every day and drink piña coladas every night and we would never, never, never look back. I'm a good southern girl. I don't tend to get in people's faces. So I let him talk while I silently wept. His dreams broke my heart. His inability to stop betraying his wife tore me to shreds. I asked that female God who had looked after me so many times to forgive me for having been—even unknowingly and briefly—a TOW.

Finally, I found my voice. "Sure, sweetie, that's exactly what will happen."

He sighed as if momentarily at peace.

That was nearly two years ago. For a while he continued to call, but I didn't pick up. I listened to his messages, though, hoping to hear some sign of redemption, some tonal quality or turn of phrase that would tell me he finally filled that hole in his pocket that made him cheat, that made him restless, that made him profoundly unhappy with himself.

By the time my year of living dangerously had come to an end, I had sworn off men. I was sick of what appeared to be their incessant need to screw every skirt that walked by. I was sick of the colleague who said how surprised he was at the ease with which women betray other women and who then propositioned me. I was sick about a married writer who, after an event, as he was driving me to his house for a party, made sure I wasn't dating anyone and then suggested I give him a blow job in the car. Besides the bold absurdity of the proposition, evidently he felt it was okay to screw around, even though he was married, as long as I was single. And I'm sure if I had agreed he would have greeted his wife with a bear hug and a kiss just as he did after I told him to fuck off.

Then there is my friend—a male—who is involved in a self-proclaimed "emotional affair" with a woman. He swears they do everything but have sex and that makes it A-ok. (By the way, I don't believe him; I've seen them on the dance floor.) They figured out that they could spend more time together if they made friends with each other's spouses. That way, cheaters and hoodwinked alike could hang out together like one fantabulous all-American family. The paramour even baby-sits my friend's children. I cannot believe his wife, who is a very smart woman, doesn't suspect. But maybe she doesn't want to. Maybe for her the prospect of keeping her family together is worth the pain and humiliation inflicted by her husband's so-called affair of the heart.

But back to the end days of my year of living dangerously. With my newfound knowledge that men cheat as easily as they chew—which means that women, despite what they say, are eager players in the infidelity game—and with my heart still broken over my failed marriage and sad attempt at a new relationship that had turned me into a TOW, I stepped anew into the world with every intention of going it alone. But my female God has a sense of humor. As soon as I closed the door to relationships, she flung it open and ushered into my life a man who felt the same way I did: Never again.

So, yes, we're together. It has been almost a year—a truly wonderful year—abundant with hope and growth, laughter and tears, and tons of really good sex. I admit to being scared, watchful. I'm not an innocent anymore. I'm wary and battle hardened. I know if he cheats on me, I will be devastated. And the TOW involved should pray she's in better than I am with our thrice-jilted God because I am one fed-up woman. I mean, is it really that difficult to keep your dick in your pants? And do we, as women, really have such low self-esteem that we're willing to screw over our fellow sisters and put out on the basis of a lie delivered on the wings of a smile? Why are we so willing to believe him when he says he is going to leave his wife? The stats are in: Even if he does leave her, he's not likely to end up with TOW because, once the marriage is over, TOW is no longer a fantasy (sex without ties); she's a home wrecker.

I think men know something about us that we don't own up to: Whether we are one-night stands or long-term TOWs, we allow ourselves to be relegated to a state of second-class anonymity because we don't respect ourselves enough to demand full citizenship where love and fidelity are concerned. That means we're victimizing ourselves. My colleague was right—women are betraying each other; it's as if we're slugging it out in a biker-girl brawl; the winner gets to claim hers is the pussy of choice, while the men enjoy all the spoils.

If I find myself once more being punked, I will be, as I said, devastated. But I will also hold all parties, including myself, accountable. I will walk if I want to, or stay if that suits my needs, but I will never again be silent or complacent. As if I am a hormonal Joan of Arc, I will bring the shame, the hurt, the tawdriness into the light so we can figure it out—how it happened, why it happened, if anything can be salvaged. That was my mistake in the past: I never dragged any of the ugliness into the sunshine.

I can't control the behavior of others and, while I might ask for faithfulness, there are no guarantees I'll get it. Life, as they say, happens. But I can demand of myself that I live honorably, that I respect myself, that I do not repeat my mother's mistakes or sins, that I never again become a door mat for a man or his TOW. I can have both compassion and disgust for TOWs and the men they bed down, but I will never again allow their behavior to stain my door permanently. I'm not sure what my methods of ascension will be, but I promise you, come hell or high water, if TOW steps back into my life, her anonymity—and his cheating ways—will be blown asunder.

Now that I think about it, TOWs might have more in common with vampires than unknown soldiers. They're both eternal (has there ever been a time on earth when TOWs did not exist?). They both have parasitic tendencies. And they share an aversion to dawn. When light ferrets them out of the shadows, vampires combust and TOWs lose all honor.

Ladies, we know the drill, so why don't we smarten up? Until we do, men will be men, boys will be boys, and The Other Woman, just like a vampire, will be cursed, forced to carry the burden of infidelity's bloodred shame all by her lonesome.

RUBY

▼

Gayle Brandeis

Shortly after we met, Matt and I were driving to a burrito stand when the song "Ruby" by Steely Dan came on the radio.

"You remind me of someone I know named Ruby," Matt said, squeezing my thigh to the beat of the music. "I've had a crush on her, like, forever."

Ruby was the best friend of his best friend's sister, he told me. He had known her, idolized her, since he was twelve. When she got married, his heart was broken. I felt a stab of jealousy, but didn't say anything. Our relationship was too new; I had no claim over him. I wasn't sure whether to be flattered or nervous that I reminded him of this woman he had put on a pedestal. I hoped he liked me for me, and not just because I was some sort of Ruby-clone. As we drove down the street, Donald Fagen continued to pine for Ruby on the radio, wondering when she would be his.

Matt's sister, Heather, lived down the hall from me in my dorm; Matt and I met when he came out to visit her at the beginning of the school year. People were slam-dancing to Led Zeppelin in Heather's room; from the time Matt and I first crashed into each other, it was hard to pry us apart. We moved into an apartment together three months later. I was nineteen, a sophomore at the University of Redlands; he was twenty-three, a construction worker. A lot of my friends were upset. They thought he wasn't "good enough" for me—I deserved an academic, they said. A scholar. But I knew Matt was smart. Brilliant, even. And what we had was very good, especially on a physical level.

My parents, to their credit, were wary but accepting of their daughter's shacking up with someone they hadn't even met. They asked me to come home to Chicago for the summer. I missed my family, but didn't want to spend too much time away from Matt. We agreed that I'd spend the first half of June with them and then head back to California to play house. The day before I left, Matt and I moseyed around San Diego. We went to the zoo and watched an orangutan pee into its own mouth, we touched 100-year-old tortoises and rode on the back of an elephant. Then we stopped at the house of one of his friends from his ski-bum days at Mammoth Mountain.

As his friend showed us the hydroponic pot farm in his walk-in closet, Matt told him, eyebrows raised, "You know,

Ruby got divorced." Ruby and her husband had lived at Mammoth part time while Matt was there. For all I knew, Matt had moved up there so he could be close to her. This was the first I had heard of her divorce. Matt's friend didn't seem too impressed by the news, but Matt sounded excited. Inordinately so. The humid closet with its garbage bag–covered window suddenly felt way too stuffy. I stepped outside to get some air.

While I was in Chicago, I talked to Matt as often as I could. He said that he was spending a lot of time with old friends—he rattled off their names, and then said casually, as if an afterthought, "Oh, and Ruby." I tried not to worry too much about this. Then, a few days before I flew back, he told me he was going to spend the weekend at his friend's family cabin up at Lake Arrowhead. Again, he rattled off a list of names. Again, he ended it with "Oh, and Ruby." I swallowed hard and told him I loved him and would see him soon.

Matt seemed distracted when he picked me up at the airport. I had built up a strong hunger for him while I was gone, but I couldn't taste that same hunger when we kissed. We stopped at Cha Cha's, our favorite burrito stand, to pick up lunch on the way back to our apartment. I sat in the passenger seat of his old Ford truck with a foil-wrapped bean, rice, and cheese burrito the size of a baby warming my lap, the tang of grapefruit ade on my tongue; I was so happy to be back in California, next to Matt. When I ran my hand up the inside of his arm, though, a move that usually made him sigh, I could feel his muscles stiffen under my touch. *It's nothing,* I tried to tell myself. *He just has to get used to me again.* We got back to our apartment and I was relieved and delighted to find that our bodies fit together just as perfectly as they always had.

A couple of days later, Matt and I were lazily kissing on the living room floor when he pulled back and said, "You're so good."

"So are you," I said, but when I leaned toward him to kiss him some more, he sat up and said, "No, I'm not."

"Yes, you are," I said playfully, thinking this was the start of one of our verbal games.

"No," he repeated. "I'm not." The tone of his voice stopped me cold.

"What are you talking about?" I asked, shivers coursing down my arms and chest.

He took a deep breath. "I fell in love with someone else while you were gone."

Ruby. The name burst in my head like a blood vessel before he even said it out loud. *Ruby. Ruby. Ruby.*

I had never been seized by such instant nausea in my life. My stomach did a good job of trying to crawl out of my mouth. I doubled over. If he had said "I slept with someone else while you were gone," or "fucked" or "screwed" or any other concrete physical verb, it would have hurt, but it wouldn't have packed the same wallop as "fell in love." The fact that it was Ruby made things even worse; I knew the pull she had on his heart. I had only been gone for two weeks, but he had been wanting her for over a decade. That's a lot of longing waiting to spill. I think he half expected me to be happy for him.

"What are you going to do?" I asked, my face between my knees.

"I don't know," he said, and both of us started to cry. "I still want to be with you, but I want to be with her, too."

And then there was nothing left for us to do but have stupid, hot, carpet-burn-inducing sex right there on the living room floor.

In the interest of "telling the truth," Matt told me way more than I wanted to know about his time with Ruby. I found out that they had done it in the lake. That they had done it quietly in a room in the cabin where his sister was doing it quietly with a boy I had had a one-night stand with shortly before I met Matt. I found out that Ruby had really enjoyed all the fun lamps—lava and fiber optic and disco—I had bought for our living room. I had no idea what Ruby looked like (other than the fact that she was "tiny," and that she, like me, had long brown curly hair), but that didn't stop me from picturing them having sex on every surface of our apartment, colored lights flashing on their skin. I became obsessed by the fact that Matt, loving wordplay, probably had fun with the subject of "Ruby's boobies." The dumb rhyme tormented me—I would be doing okay and suddenly "Ruby's boobies" would pop into my head and throw me into a pit of despair.

Matt had gotten violently sunburned as he lay with Ruby on the deck at Lake Arrowhead. I spent what felt like endless hours peeling the skin off his back. Sometimes it came off in great satisfying sheets; sometimes it came off in tiny dandruff-like flakes. I didn't really care how it came off, though, as long as it disappeared. I wanted to get rid of the skin that she had seen, the skin that she had touched. I wanted to get down to the raw pink skin that only I would know.

When we had sex, sometimes I tried to forget we were Matt and Gayle. I tried to think of us as just Man and Woman, turning us into pure bodies, stripping any story from our coupling. Otherwise, I would want to cry. Otherwise, the anger would get too great for any pleasure to surge through. I don't quite know why I stayed. I thought many times of leaving. But some stubborn part of me wasn't ready to give up yet. Some ruthless part of me wondered whether I had the power to win him fully back.

The anger flared up at night. I found myself weeping regularly at three in the morning. I found myself kicking Matt in his sleep, pummeling his back, pulling his hair. He would wake up, startled, and I'd sob at him, and he'd try to calm me down. I had a dream where I strangled a woman with leopard skin and dark hair hanging down her back. I knew it was Ruby. I used a thick chain. It was the most satisfying dream I had ever had in my life.

I was grateful that Ruby was out of town my first weeks back in California; she had gone up to a festival in Oregon with a friend. One day we received a box from her, addressed to both Matt and me. I opened it before Matt got home. It was full of summer fruit and a T-shirt saying I ♥ ORGANIC. It pained me to know that if she weren't my rival for Matt,

I would probably like this girl. There was also a card decorated with fairies, inscribed with a single sentence: "It's been a magical experience." I wondered if she wanted the message to sound ambiguous—maybe she wanted me to think she meant the festival in Oregon, but she wanted Matt to know she meant their time together. If so, I was on to her tricks. I gorged myself on almost every plum and apricot and peach in the box, practically choking on them, barely tasting their sweetness. When I couldn't handle another bite, I threw the rest of the fruit off our second-floor balcony and watched it fall with one satisfying splat after another on the ground below. I didn't want Matt to eat a single piece of fruit that Ruby had touched. I didn't even want him to see those lush ripe globes. I took the T-shirt to Goodwill. I ripped up the card, tossed the box. By the time Matt got home, it was as if she hadn't sent a thing.

Of course, I couldn't erase her as easily from our lives. On the Fourth of July, Matt told me he had plans to spend the day with her. I swallowed my panic and wrote a letter for him to give her, one that essentially said that I didn't ever want to meet her, but I wished her well. Actually, in trying to seem spiritual and magnanimous, I wrote, "I wish you Nirvana" (secretly hoping that my apparent open-heartedness would guilt her away from Matt). He drove out to Orange County and I tried not to freak out too much. If Matt was going to be a jerk, who needed him? I told myself I needed to be my own woman. I needed to celebrate my own Declaration of Independence from him and his idiocy. So I went to a Girl Scout–run festival at the park down the street. I tossed bean bags through holes and ate cotton candy and stood in line to make spin art. I squirted purple and green and yellow and pink paint onto a spinning piece of paper and told myself that the colorful, smeary, mandala I created was an emblem of my autonomy. It was something I could always look at and be reminded of my own strength. I went to a dumb Chevy Chase movie and laughed my head off. I went to the fireworks display on campus and lay on the grass and felt a real kinship with all that broken sparkle in the air.

When I got back to the apartment, feeling powerful and free and just about resolved to leave Matt and head back to Chicago, I found Matt in the dark bedroom, crying.

"She had a date," he told me, one arm flung over his eyes. He said he had hung out with her all day, but then after she showered (did he shower with her? did he touch *Ruby's boobies?*) and started putting on makeup, she told him she was going out to dinner with someone else. He felt as if she had kicked him in the gut.

"Do you expect me to feel sorry for you?" I asked, incredulous.

He shook his head. "I'm the sorry one," he said. "If I ever made you feel the way I feel right now, I'm so sorry."

He had made me feel a whole lot worse than that, I thought, but I could feel my heart starting to thaw. I crawled into bed with him, and we did what we could to comfort one another. I found myself flooded with a sense of relief, tinged with a tentative rush of victory.

Ruby continued to haunt our relationship. Her number

showed up on our phone bills, long, expensive conversations, in sporadic fits for several months. Matt would drive out to see her every once in a while (leaving notes saying things like *I went to visit Doug. Oh, and Ruby*). He told me they weren't having sex anymore, and I wanted to believe him, but I wasn't sure I could.

For our first anniversary as a couple, I signed us up for hang-gliding lessons, thinking it could be a way for us to leave the past behind and fly into our future together. It didn't quite have its intended effect—I sucked at the sport and wanted nothing more to do with it, but hang-gliding quickly became Matt's passion, his avocation (even his vocation for a brief while). At some point, he invited Ruby to go on a tandem ride with him, which felt like a slap in the face. To my relief, she called to say she couldn't make it. I was the one who answered the phone; it was the first time I had heard her voice. It was just a normal voice. A human voice. Not some chiming, perfect-goddess voice. This came as a relief. Still, I fell into a quivering, teary heap after our short, civil conversation ended. Once I collected myself, though, I felt empty, cleansed, strong. I had survived the call. I had survived what I hoped was the whole sordid Ruby ordeal.

A few weeks later, Matt and I were skinny-dipping with his sister and the boy I had the brief fling with, the boy who had been part of Matt and Ruby's Lake Arrowhead adventure. "You're the only one for me," Matt told me, our bodies twining under water, slippery as eels. "I don't know how I ever could have thought otherwise." Hearing that felt so good. Hearing it with witnesses on hand, witnesses who had seen him with Ruby, somehow made it feel even better.

Matt did what he could to earn back my trust. He wrote *I love you* on the wall of our shower with hair. He stopped calling Ruby. He made an effort not to pay attention to other women. He made an even greater effort to let me know how much he appreciated me and my patience with him. He said he would make it worth my while, and he did. We got engaged about a year later. I got pregnant less than a year after that, and we married a bit earlier than we had planned. Three years later, we had our second baby. I was (and am) deeply grateful for the family, the life, we created together.

As happy as Matt and I were together, it took me a long time to fully get over the Ruby situation. For years, I couldn't hear the word "ruby" in any context without crying. Days were ruined over the silliest thing: walking down a long pier, only to find a diner named Ruby's at the end of it; seeing a raw, unpolished ruby in an exhibit of minerals and gems at a museum; hearing Glinda ask Dorothy to click her ruby slippers together, all stabbed me straight in the heart. Matt tried to protect me—he even ushered me out of a music venue when Steely Dan's "Ruby" started to come over the loudspeakers—but sometimes I would get engulfed by waves of anger and pain. Every once in a while we'd have to go through the whole late-night cry-and-apologize cycle again, sometimes even preceded by the kick-Matt-in-his-sleep cycle. Matt often assured me that if the Ruby affair had to happen, it was good that it happened before we were married, before we had kids. He got straying out of his system early, he said. He'd never have to look elsewhere again. If it hadn't have happened, he said, he might not have learned how much I meant to him. I believed him and trusted him, but it seemed like a stupid way to learn a lesson. The wounds still ran deep.

I avoided any events where I knew Ruby might be present. This frustrated Matt greatly; he wanted his childhood friends to know me. As much as he understood my reasons, he felt I was denying him a large and important part of his life. He tried to convince me to go to weddings and parties in his old neighborhood, but I wound up staying home with the kids more often than not. In the meanwhile, Ruby had gotten married to the man she had the date with on that Fourth of July. Matt reported that she and her husband were both wearing rhinestone "Jesus" pins on their jacket lapels at a friend's party. This reassured me more than anything else, somehow.

When Matt's best friend's wedding came around, I knew I couldn't miss it. It was way too important an occasion for me to let my own discomfort get in the way, even though Ruby would be there for sure—she was still Matt's best friend's sister's best friend. It had been sixteen years since she and Matt had had their fling, but I was still nervous to see her. I worried that all my old visions of *Ruby's boobies*, of the two of them entwined, would come flooding back, would maybe even be intensified, once I could visualize her more clearly. I bought the hottest dress I could find, a sexy black beaded number, and tried to psych myself up.

As we walked into the church for the ceremony, Matt bent over and whispered "That's Ruby." Her name sent an electric shock through my body. Tears sprang into my eyes. I almost couldn't look, but I forced myself to, and I found myself flooded with the same relief I had felt when I first heard her voice: She wasn't some goddess, she was a person. Kind of short. Long curly hair. Big eyes. Pretty, but not in any disconcerting way. She wore a modest red sweater, a modest gray skirt. She had two toddlers in tow. This was her. This was the woman who had haunted my dreams, whose name had caused such turmoil. How could I have given her so much power? Years of angst lifted from my chest at once. I slipped into a pew with Matt, leaned against him, and took a deep breath. He was mine. I am not competitive by nature, but one phrase wouldn't stop going through my head: *I won.* A much better mantra than *Ruby's boobies*, to be sure.

Later, at the reception, I danced as I had never danced before. I went totally wild, jumping around, flinging my hips, tossing my head so my hair flew in every direction. I felt like a madwoman. I felt utterly free. If Ruby got too close to us on the dance floor, Matt, who was now much more nervous than I about any potential run-ins, would try to steer us away, but I just danced even harder. I gave Matt a huge kiss and we danced all night long.

IN PRAISE OF MARRIED MEN
▼

Susan Cheever

The first married man I ever slept with was the one who was married to me—my first husband. The second married man I slept with was married to someone else.

With the first one, after a honeymoon and blaze of passion and desire, we settled into a life of pleasant routine. Over a few years, that routine gave way to mutual irritation and lack of appreciation. We owned each other, so we could relax. We didn't bother to dress for each other or to keep each other away from our most repulsive and intimate grooming rituals; he watched me tweeze my eyebrows, I saw him deal with his hemorrhoids. We merged all of our possessions, and the books I had treasured in college, D. H. Lawrence and e. e. cummings, got lost in the bookcases dominated by his history obsession. The little salad bowl I had brought from a trip to the Bahamas was stowed on a back shelf because his salad bowl was much,

much nicer. He made the money, but I handled it and planned our budget each week. I gave him an allowance for lunch at his Fifth Avenue magazine office—a cause of much hilarity among his friends. We told each other everything. I said that his children annoyed me. I told him that I had married him and that I did not intend to help with them. I complained when they were coming to visit and sulked while they were in residence. I hated his parents and they hated me. He was a writer and editor and when I read something he had written I told him exactly what I thought of it. The results were explosive. I accused him of being unable to take criticism. After a few years, I stopped reading most of what he wrote. Who could blame me? He accused me of failing to take him seriously. Since my life was all about taking care of him—or so it seemed to me—I didn't see why I should have to take him seriously on top of that. I disliked his friends, who were older and seemed pretentious; he thought my friends were silly girls and often forgot their names. After a while, we took each other for granted, and after that we began to think of each other as heavy weights holding us back from the wonderful lives we deserved.

But with someone else's husband, everything was quite different. The first time it happened my excitement was balanced by guilt. His wife was a friend of mine and I knew that sleeping with her husband was not a friendly thing to do. She was in another city, though, and our instant, passionate connection seemed to exist in its own time and place. When we were together, the world fell away; those times were the most vivid and longed-for days in my life. I looked my best; I turned on all my wit and facility with words. It was my pleasure to make him laugh out loud. I set my charm to stun. I often prepared for telephone conversations with this man by making lists of topics and jokes. When he gave me something to read that he had written, I studied it as if it were the key to happiness and told him what a genius he was. If I had suggestions, I couched them in respectful and positive terms. He returned the favor.

It was hard to get my own husband's attention. When I walked into a room or when I picked him up at his office, he rarely commented on what I was wearing or how I looked. Sometimes when he did comment, I would wish he had not. When I complained, he said he was trying to be honest. He only occasionally seemed glad to see me. He asked about what was for dinner; he wanted to know if I had gotten the car fixed or if I had completed one of the dozens of domestic errands he considered my responsibility.

With the other woman's husband, the situation was reversed. When I walked into a restaurant or a bar where I was meeting him, his face lit up. "I can't believe you're really here," he would say. A touch from him was electrifying. Sex was bliss, a delicious tangle of long-delayed desires and a sense of adventure fostered by the secrecy and rarity of our lovemaking.

Some of my friends disapproved, and I heard over and over that married men never left their wives and that I was wasting myself on a man who would not be available to build a life with me. I didn't care. I didn't feel responsible for the disintegration of anyone else's marriage. We were all adults, I was fond of saying. Could I help it if my soul mate happened to be inconveniently married to someone else? The intense pleasure and connection I experienced with this man seemed worth anything I had to give up. I didn't think about how I would manage to have children or create my own family or build a life. I lived in the moment, and they were glorious moments.

I remember one night in particular when I told my husband that I was going to a boring party with my friends—many of whom were his friends—and I secretly arranged to meet someone else's husband in the lobby of the building where the party was being held. I planned to stay at the party just long enough so that my presence there would register. "I was at Vivian's party!" I could say, but I planned to leave early enough so that I could steal two or three hours with someone else's husband before I had to be home. I arrived to find that it was a crowded party in a Soho loft with an elevator that opened right into the living room. Disaster. Everyone would see me go. Someone might notice the time and casually report it to my husband.

For cover, I enlisted the help of a friend. I took her into a corner and explained the situation and asked her to chat with me in front of the elevator and then move away as I got in, as if our conversation had ended—that way, at least there would be a distraction. I asked her if she thought I was doing something wrong. She shrugged. "Men do this all the time," she said.

Eventually, I divorced my husband and married the man who had been someone else's husband when I met him. (My friends were wrong; he did leave his wife.) Call me stupid—I'm sure you have called me many names by now, if you are still reading this essay—but I was astonished when the same thing began to happen between us that had happened with my first husband. For a few years we were exhilarated and thrilled to be together. Slowly, the magic wore off. We merged our books and possessions. We stopped taking care to appear our best. We began to complain about each other's friends and family. We squabbled over money. We squabbled over everything. For me, the solution was obvious: I began cheating on my new husband with someone else's husband.

It took me a long time to realize that sleeping with married men didn't work for me. I mean it took decades. It took two marriages and a series of affairs and a tsunami of emotional destruction, some of which, to my lasting regret and shame, was visited on my young daughter. First, I came to see that it wasn't practical: I didn't really know the men I was in love with because they were married to someone else and this distorted them. Second, it wasn't possible to make a sensible choice about marriage while blinded by a passion for a situation that was temporary.

Then I began to see, through the fog of my desire, that there were moral problems as well. It wasn't enough of an excuse to say that "men do this all the time." It wasn't enough to think that, since everyone said that married men never left their wives, I wasn't hurting a marriage; they did leave their wives. It wasn't enough to say that we were all adults or that I wasn't lying to anyone. By being part of a situation that was a lie—even if the man did all the actual lying—I was lying as surely as if I made the calls to say that I would be late at work or that I had been held up in traffic or that I had two days of business out of town.

I gave up married men. It was hard to do, and I found that it became easier when I had nothing to do with attractive men who were married to other women. I didn't have lunch with them or answer their calls. Most of all, I did not discuss with them the reasons why I couldn't sleep with them. Experience had taught me that this particular kind of conversation inevitably led to hot, explosive sex.

My turning point came one day when I heedlessly accepted a ride from Easthampton, Long Island, where I had spent a day with friends, to New York City, with the husband of a woman I knew. We got along famously. We made each other laugh and soon he was making points with a touch on my arm or a squeeze of my shoulder. These touches felt electric. We stopped for gas. We both got out of the car and I headed for the ladies' room. When I returned he was standing, holding the passenger door open for me and smiling. Our bodies came within inches as I slid back into the car. I knew what was going to happen. I could almost see us tangled in the sheets of one of the motels just off the Long Island Expressway.

We got back in the car and started talking again, but now we talked about passion between two people. It was the kind of dangerous conversation I had promised myself I would avoid, but it seemed to be taking me over. I stood at a crossroads. How could I stop? Something outside myself told me what to do; I began bragging about my children. I told this sexy man about my daughter's writing contest and my son's adorable way of pronouncing the word *breakfast*. As I spoke, I could feel the man's attention drift. Even more miraculously, I could feel myself returning to sanity. The more I talked about my kids, the more I remembered myself as a responsible woman, a mother, not the kind of person who pulls off the highway for a quickie on the way home.

"What would you do if you had ten thousand dollars and four days and you had to spend it on yourself?" he asked, changing the subject away from my kids. I knew what he meant. I flashed a bedroom at the Hôtel du Cap in Antibes. That's where we would go. I imagined the weekend, the excuses, lying there with him as the fragrant Mediterranean air wafted in through the casement windows and the sound of a faraway tennis game floated in from the gardens that run down to the sea.

"I'd spend it on the kids," I said. "A new bicycle, some tutoring, a cool summer camp, something like that." An hour later, when he dropped me off at home, it was over. He didn't even lean in for a good-bye kiss.

There are many explanations for why I was so attracted to married men. Perhaps it was because way back when

I was a little girl I had wanted to steal my father away from my mother. In fact, I had quite a lot of luck taking my father away from my mother; theirs was not a happy marriage and I often went with my father as his date to literary events or to lunch or dinner with friends. Or perhaps I was afraid of intimacy and could only be attracted to men who were not available. Sometimes I thought I might secretly be in love with the wives of the men I slept with—they were often formidable and beautiful women.

Looking back on those years, I can see that I was also attracted to married men for very good reasons. As a mistress, I was able to stay in possession of my own life. I had freedom; I had my own place; there was no merging of books or friends. As a mistress, I was my lover's fantasy and he was mine; the intensity of fantasy and the creativity of fantasy were poured into making our time together brilliant with pleasure and luminous with desire. "He put me on a pedestal," says one friend who recently had a married lover. "He treated me like a queen."

As a mistress, I could live my own life—pursue my career, spend time with my friends, even stay up all night reading—at the same time knowing that I was beloved and fascinating to someone. I was able to love married men not because they were available or because they reminded me of Daddy, but because they allowed me to be myself and to live in the world of my friends and family who nurtured and protected me. There is little possessiveness in a married man; he doesn't have the right. Of course,

I couldn't be possessive either—a married lover is already possessed.

In the end, the moral and practical reasons for not sleeping with other women's husbands prevail. Adultery is the subject of one of the ten commandments, after all. I have even come to disapprove slightly when other women do it, although I have to remind myself of my own history. Still, if I ever marry again, I would like to marry someone who can act as if he is married to someone else, even though he may be my husband. I would like to treat and be treated with the kind of passionate respect I remember from having married lovers. I would like to live in the moment. I don't want to merge lives and expose everything. I have no desire to tell unpleasant truths or to hear them. If I ever marry again, I would like to find a husband who acts as if he is married to someone else—even though that someone else is me.

SHEBA

▼

Sherry Glaser

August 1999

I'd been invited to teach a workshop on radical emotional transformation at the first annual Goddess Gather, a three-day event for women held on the Mendocino Coast. I was also slated to perform my one-woman comedy show, *Oh My Goddess!* My goal was to behave and focus on my work, instead of on the beautiful women who surrounded me. But how could I do that, when I have an extremely potent libido and am notoriously incestuous with women I meet under circumstances like these?

I walked out on the porch of the old farmhouse to meet and mingle.

She caught my eye and wouldn't let go. Hmm? Who's that? Here was a woman, though not all would agree at first glance. She stood over six feet tall and was leaning against the porch railing in the August sunlight. Her hair. Her hair cascaded down her back and shoulders, shocks of pure white with long streaks of black and gray. It was unlike any mane I'd ever seen, even on a horse. Her wide nostrils flared with power; I expected her to rear up and whinny. And she had a billy goat's gruff—a beard. The bearded lady. Her left arm was dramatically tattooed with an undersea paradise of green and blue waves, mermaid, treasure chest, and whale. Someone called out "Sheba!" and she turned around.

We were summoned by the Cosmic Priestess for the first workshop, called into a circle and instructed to sit with our opposite astrological signs. I am a Gemini, born on June 7. "Sagittarius," announced Sheba, and my heart jumped! She crawled across the room in my direction, shimmied up against my legs, which I opened so she could get more comfortable. She asked if I minded. "No, I don't mind." She laid her gorgeous head in my lap. I couldn't stop my hands from stroking, though out of respect I still asked, "May I touch your hair?" and she said, "Oh, yeah." Her hair was strong like flax and smooth as seaweed fresh from the ocean. She smelled like sacred plants: tobacco, cannabis, and sandalwood smoldering between my legs. I was getting lost in pheromones. I couldn't help but fantasize what her big paws would feel like around my body. I reminded myself that I was there on business. Besides, I already had a girlfriend who was also the nanny for my children, and Sheba had brought an entourage from San Francisco. Was one of them her lover? Perhaps she was their den mother.

Throughout the weekend, we would bump into each other or sneak glimpses. She participated in my workshop and sat in my audience, but neither of us would confess our attraction. We parted with customary and courteous hugs and farewells.

I saw Sheba from time to time at community gatherings, peace demonstrations, and drum circles. While we were always otherwise engaged, we remained on a parallel course. I heard stories from mutual friends that she was a philanthropist, an alchemist, an angel of mercy, a hedonist, and a student of ancient mysteries. She seemed so remote, legendary, really, and I had so many things on my plate; I could eat only what was on it.

Four years later, I heard that Sheba and her girlfriend had moved into a cabin a couple of miles down the road from me. It's a country road that dead-ends; in order to go anywhere, she had to drive by my house. My girlfriend, Birdy, had been around for a few years, having come into my life when I was in deep crisis. My mother, who lived across the country, had fallen deathly ill; my life was in chaos. I needed comfort, help, and company. Birdy offered this, as well as her services as personal assistant and sound designer. She had been a fan of my work for years and had fantasized about making a life with me. She started with such enthusiasm, devotion, and energy. I thought she might be a good butch wife; she had the potential. I decided to give men up for a while and try to be a full-time lesbian.

I'd been bisexual for years, not wanting to limit myself

to one gender in the search for my perfect mate. There were some aspects of the male species I really enjoyed but, in my experience, lesbians have more fun. Women are my favorite people to hang out with. You know that closeness you feel with your best friend? That translates to physical intimacy. It's the common ground of knowing how your lover feels when she's about to bleed, or her shame around fat thighs, a yeast infection, or the all-too-common heartbreak of sexual abuse. You can make love to those deep wounds and watch them heal. The soft flesh reflects the vulnerable heart. There's the laughter, the familiarity, the trust; and not only that, but sex between women is completely unlimited. Our capacity for pleasure has no end. If we want to, we can have orgasms all day and night. It's an amazing thrill to give a woman an orgasm. You're basically giving her what you want yourself.

I had been with a few women, but I never really got to trim my nails on a regular basis. (The sound of a fingernail clipper is one of the most erotic sounds in the lesbian bedroom. It means that your lover wants to be inside you and her consideration is paramount, making sure she has no sharp or jagged edges on her tender fingertips.) The women I had been with were pretty much novice lesbians, and sex was intermittent. Birdy had more experience than I, but something went wrong. There can be danger in such profound intimacy because the original, primary pain of one's life tends to surface. If you do not have navigational skills, you can drown in the raging emotional river you've just dredged.

After six months of that hot "throw you up against the wall and fuck you silly," Birdy and I were in the sorry state of eternal processing. She began to slur her words as her Prozac levels would dip and climb. Something was eating her and she began to shrink before my eyes. Conditions of disintegration and wasting were whittling her down to brittle bones. We clung to the hope that somehow we could recover our passion, staying together in spite of the recurring drama.

I could recite ahead of time what the routine of the night would be when Birdy came over. She would start out looking wounded and soft and grab me tighter than her arms could bear, as if to make sure I was still hers, her breath rancid from indigestion, tobacco, and medications I couldn't pronounce. Then the natural chaos of the evening would begin, with my youngest daughter banging out "Heart and Soul" on the piano ten or fifteen times. The phone would constantly ring and my teenager didn't know how to shut a door without slamming it. Birdy would take refuge on the front porch with her cigarettes. She wouldn't be able to eat the succulent meal I had prepared because her stomach was tied up in knots, but then we'd fight because I couldn't stand that she could smoke but not eat. She would try to defend herself and then leave, afraid to explode in my face. Then she would call and we would process for an hour and she would promise to return, only to fall asleep in her own bed from exhaustion.

Sheba's girlfriend was also a handful. In fact, it turned out that both our girlfriends had chronic illnesses and were known to lie, steal, and cheat to acquire their beloved opiates. People constantly informed me that Birdy had asked them for free samples of their prescriptions. She vigorously denied this and I believed her. All she needed was my love and everything would be well. I would save her.

That summer, Sheba took up the habit of coming by every other Wednesday to see if my trash needed disposal. She loved that task, getting dirty as she sorted through the recycling and hoisted the huge cans into her truck. I felt a quickening every time she appeared in the driveway: a bit of fear, a spark of desire. I couldn't really look into her eyes when I thanked her because her gaze was so intense. What on earth did she want?

One crisp fall morning, Sheba stopped by and asked me to have breakfast with her down the coast. She made it seem so casual. It wasn't a date, more of a spontaneous get-together. The conversation over the wild mushroom frittata had that familiar riff of "Yeah, my girlfriend, she's got problems" and "I'm unhappy, but we've been together so long." And you get all excited because you know exactly what's wrong with your girlfriend and you would never do anything the way she does it and it's so simple...gosh. There's that thrilling, unspoken dialogue of "we're meant for each other, honey."

But we still weren't ready to run off with each other because we held all the power in relationships where we could keep vigil over those who could never know as much as we did, never love as well as we could, never be who we would eventually be: our whole selves. We forgave the larceny, the car crashes, the slit tires, aiding and *abedding* the enemy who claimed sovereignty, tenure forever. After breakfast, we went into a little shop and Sheba bought me the softest brown sweater ever. I pretty much wore it every day.

On those trash days, Sheba would occasionally smoke a cigarette on the back deck with me. The way she inhaled that cigarette was dangerously sexy. Her big, strong, well-manicured fingers drawing the cigarette to her lips. *No, don't look at her lips, you've got a girlfriend. Sure, she's a foot shorter and not half as cute, but she's yours and you are loyal and should not be looking at those lips because then you'll start looking at her beard.*

I couldn't help look at her beard. I ask you, when do you see a beard on a woman? Sometimes you can see the shadow where a beard would like to be but, in this culture, she wouldn't dare, unless she was Sheba. I like men with beards. I like the softness of the hair, rather than the stubble of their chin. But with Sheba I could imagine not only her chin hair being soft, but the skin next to it. Soft, like mine.

Whenever Sheba was excited about something, she would do a jig of sorts. She would bounce her hefty six-foot frame and jump from toe to toe. Adorable. I finally asked her why she came around, what did she want? She said, point blank, "I want to fuck you." Uh-oh. I giggled nervously at the thought, but quickly dismissed it as a flirtation and sent her on her way.

It never occurred to me that I would be ripe pickings for Sheba, that I would have the capacity to handle that much sexuality, power, desire. She scared me. She started seeping into my daily consciousness. She was nasty cute in her defiant T-shirts that said I MAKE BOYS CRY or FUCK YOU, YOU FUCKING FUCK. She didn't give a shit about what anybody thought. That scared me in the most exciting way. I secretly wanted to be her femme. Sheba was like a giant or, as my younger child referred to her, "a big fluffy bunny" who rode on sturdy pillars of voluptuous thighs.

It was a wet winter and I walked in the woods in my high boots, my hounds at my side. The smell of conifers, redwood, and mud is thrilling to me. It makes me swell with inspiration. The forest turns me on. It makes me ripe and juicy. Hiking with my lover through the woods is erotically thrilling to me, but every day I found myself alone because Birdy didn't have the energy to take a walk. My primal sexual instincts rumbled through my bones as I swished through the wild and called out my lover's name: Birdy. Her name clipped through my lips, cut short by the y at the end; it sounded like a wheel that needed WD-40. There was no satisfaction in my longing; her name stuck in my teeth like a popcorn kernel. But when I dared even to whisper the other woman's name, my secret desire, the sweet wind whistled through my lips. "Sh, Shh, Shh, sexy. Shhh, Shhh." She, the epitome of her, feminine, She. The all, the complete, She, the sacred name of the Goddess who had been silenced for millennia. She, the alias, the one name that no one could say because of power unleashed, She. Sheba.

It began as a quiet call, like the air through the redwood and pine needles, but as the lyric found its melody it began to build like, well, like an orgasm. I said it. I said it again. Then I started to shout "Sheba, Sheeeeba!" The wind blew harder, as though Nature abhors a vacuum and needed to hear that kind of call. Weak branches plummeted to the ground and the ethers would deliver the message, the call: collect.

Spring introduced herself with buttery daffodils and luscious green grass from the heavy winter rains. It was the day before St. Patrick's Day and I was feeling lucky, even though I'm Jewish. It was a Wednesday, trash day. I was alone. Birdy was going to a doctor's appointment, one of many. She had been plagued by mysterious conditions and had been operated on for carpal tunnel syndrome (a dreadful situation for any good lesbian). She had left our bed early in the morning to see a specialist about her post-surgery numbness. That meant she had to borrow my car to go to San Francisco, a good 180 miles away, and wouldn't be back until late that night, or even the next morning. I was housebound.

I was just finishing a decadent goat cheese spinach omelet when I heard the engine of a mighty truck approaching. Sheba blew up my driveway in a cloud of dust. It happened that her girlfriend also had a doctor's appointment about 70 miles away and wouldn't be back for some time. I knew this because our two girlfriends had discussed the possibility of carpooling south and sharing tales of anguish and suffering. Sheba got off her horse—I mean, she got out of the truck—and went directly to the trash shack. I tried to control myself, staying busy washing the dishes, but my hands bathing in the warm water made me want her. She became my obsession. Every sound was her possible approach. After ten minutes, something happened inside me—call it possession, because the only thing I could think about was her kiss. I knew she wanted me. I had to confess I wanted her, too. Why not? Why continue the ever-painful daily routine of obligation? I wanted her and I was afraid to admit it, to claim someone who would obviously be my equal or better. How long had I asked for a love who would stand on equal ground with me, provide for herself and her family, for someone with strong heart connections in the world? Someone with power and presence, like me. A mirror.

I found myself moving toward the front door. Sheba was by the trash shack, ably lifting heavy cans onto the bed of her truck. She wore a loud Hawaiian shirt, lots of hibiscus. Her silvery hair hung in a long ponytail under the ever-present black cap. Gorgeous. There was no stopping me. I tore open the front door, marched down the steps, and started across the lawn. She looked up, but kept on with her task. When I was close enough to touch her, I stopped. Her brown eyes were fixed, direct, and I gushed, "I've got to kiss you, I just have to. Is that all right?" She said, "Yes," and closed her eyes. The combination of lust, excitement, fear, and danger was unnerving. Our kiss was restrained, a bit tentative, holding back a tremendous and possibly overwhelming passion. Some smelly garbage had soiled her hands, so she kept them to herself. But there was an undeniable buried longing, a familiar taste in her mouth, delicious.

We stopped kissing; both instantly shy, but awakened. She came in the house to wash her hands. I stood in the kitchen watching her, wondering how far we would go. Both of us had been telling our girlfriends that it was over, not going well, wanting to see other people, et cetera, but neither of them would budge. So we'd have to budge them. She dried her hands on her shirt and pulled me into her. Her arms completely surrounded me. I felt exquisitely beautiful, pure femme. She gently devoured me with her mouth and those sweet soft whiskers tickled my neck and shoulders.

Ah, the luck of the Jewish.

The next day, I explained to Birdy that not only did I want to open our relationship to others, but there was a specific other, really only one other: Sheba. I said I was going to return to non-monogamy and indulge my cravings. "You are?" asked Birdy, her eyes wide. "But will we still be close?" I said, "Of course" out of fear, rather than truth.

The next night, I brought Sheba to my bed. Our passion consumed us. It was the kind of sex I had thought was possible; it was the kind of sex I had hoped was possible. She was the embodiment of androgyny; she was the most erotic balance of nature I had ever experienced. She found me entirely intoxicating. We were stunned by pleasure; we had been waiting a long time for this undeniable chemistry to mix. At last, satisfaction.

As we lay there, fused at the belly, we heard Birdy's

little truck coming up the driveway. Sheba and I froze. Birdy walked in the front door and called out my name. I didn't answer. She came up the stairs to the bedroom and asked me to let her in. I told her no. I said, "Go home, you have to wait your turn." She insisted on coming in, that it was her bedroom too. She beat at the door. I got out of bed and Sheba pulled the sheets up around her. I threw on a robe and opened the door. "I'm sorry, you can't come in. Go home and I'll talk to you tomorrow." She cursed all the way down the stairs and slammed the front door behind her.

The next few days were painful and confusing. Birdy and I tried to share the bed again, but it was no use. Days later, she moved out.

It's been seven years since I met Sheba and a year since she moved in. Our relationship is wild, passionate, and sometimes extremely loud and dramatic. Through it all, the mirror is strong and the reflection is essential. We just got back from a two-week romance in Eastern Europe. We kissed on the bridges in Amsterdam, waltzed on a street corner in Vienna, and stayed in bed making love all day in Prague. I had never been to Europe. I've been a lot of places with Sheba I've never been. For me, there is no other.

THE *OTHER* OTHER WOMAN

▼

Nancy Weber

I was the child of a romantic marriage, the very model of a monogamous union, gorgeous and inevitable-feeling, Bogie and Bacall. Mysteriously, I was born without the monogamy gene I should have received twice over, although you can hear and see both my parents in me—I'm even blue-eyed for my mother one day and hazel-eyed like Daddy the next.

As an Eisenhower-era adolescent, I was typical enough in my immediate amorous ambitions, hoping against hope for a Saturday night date. But when I pictured the distant future of my heart, I didn't imagine myself dancing my parents' dance, attempting to re-create our near-perfect family.

If I thought of marriage, it was as the prelude to a stylish divorce. No pearly puff of a wedding dress waited for me in the shop windows of my fantasies. Instead, I obsessed over the wide-brimmed black hat I would wear to expensive lunches with my darkly handsome ex-husband, the two of us laughing and nodding knowingly, nine parts sweet to a dash of bitter.

Sometimes my fantasies dispensed with marriage altogether and I dreamed of having twelve children *à la carte* by each of the twelve greatest men alive in my time. William O. Douglas was one of them, and I seem to remember Mel Tormé. Little idiot though I was, I had taste.

Raised in an agnostic Yankee Jewish household, I both envied and despised my Catholic schoolmates' belief that certain sexual behaviors, even certain thoughts, were sinful. In my evolving ethos, the bad things were capital punishment, segregation, The Bomb, J. Edgar Hoover, Edgar Guest, and non-Bumblebee tuna, which would give you botulism—all harder to eradicate than libidinous fantasies about broody-eyed Yale sophomores.

Sex might be naughty but it wasn't bad, although it could be used badly and bad things might come of it. Across the street from my elementary school, a few minutes' walk from my parents' safe white clapboard house, stood Saint Mary's Home, a shelter for unwed mothers. It loomed large in my dreads, the more so because I never saw anyone go into or come out of the huge red brick building with its perfect apron of lawn.

I had nothing against monogamy, but I had nothing for it. Then came a defining moment.

One afternoon, when I was a senior in high school—I'm sure it was afternoon, in early fall, the light in my parents' bedroom thick and slanting—I asked my mother what she would do if my father slept with another woman. "Cut it off," she said, slicing her hand through the air in case I didn't catch her drift. It was perhaps the most shocking thing she ever said to me: my left-leaning, elegant artist mother who gave me Françoise Sagan and Henry Miller to read at a time when some of my friends were forbidden *West Side Story.*

I cannot remember why I put the question to my mother or what we said to each other afterwards. She did fancy herself a provocateur—*provocateuse*, she would have insisted—and she relished upsetting people's notions of who she was. If I dare offer this story for print (I've deleted and restored it half a dozen times), it's because she's the woman whose favorite photograph of herself, the one she asked to have preserved for her grandchildren, shows her standing tall and svelte at age sixty-something in a glamorous B. H. Wragge cocktail dress, balancing a tumbler of Dewar's on her unnaturally blond head.

She can't have meant those three dire words. I can't ever have thought she did. But how might such an impulse exist at even the farthest edge of imagination? It wasn't just the violent physical imagery; it was the elevation of sex as the holy of holies, and the implicit devaluation of everything else in a marriage. My mother's imperious surgical swipe did away with intimacies of mind and intercourse of spirit; she killed her own joy (for she loved my father madly); she pulled a Medea on my brother and me. The floodgates opened and swept our family out to sea—books and paintings and music and politics and jokes at the delicious dinner table, the us-ness of us tumbling into seaweed-strewn oblivion.

The punishment so didn't fit the hypothetical crime; I believe I was instantly remade by the injustice. I would dedicate myself to decriminalizing the offending act. Maybe the real crime was fidelity, if devotion to it could so distort a rational, civilized mind.

I didn't need analysis to know that Oedipus had visited my fevered psyche and left his mark. My parents, ever champions of my aspirations as a writer, gave me my first electric typewriter, the Smith Corona Electra, as a high-school graduation present. The warranty card asked me to check off a box explaining my reason for choosing the Electra. I checked "other" and wrote in green ink: "Because I'm in love with my father."

Showed it to my folks, who pronounced it hilarious. I ran across the street to drop the card in the mailbox, then waited for The One at Smith Corona to call and ask me out.

I was on the mistress track, clickety-clack.

The amazing thing isn't that I had an affair with one of my college professors, it's that we didn't happen until my junior year.

I had arrived on campus a virgin with nerve endings in an uproar, sure I knew everything important and eager to educate my classmates and teachers. Smoked unfiltered cigarettes, sipped Jack Daniels straight because rum and

Coke made me puke but Scotch was my mother's tipple, drank my coffee black, and filled a small three-ring binder with urgent thoughts.

Nothing is good in excess, including moderation.

The thing is to live.

Too many women I know are oval and round; I want to be a thousand corners, a geometric dream of squares and lines, corners never blunted, never sanded. I want to be a line that goes on and on and turns and moves to right and left and up and down and forward: knowing where I'm going but sometimes going somewhere else, to some new corner, darker, greater; not a circle, softly mincing, this way, that, ending up just where it started.

A mistress in the making, for sure; and came the clincher. I got an apartment in Greenwich Village, part of a sublime deal with my ever-indulgent parents. After a rocky sophomore year, and a year at the University of Geneva and surrounding cafés, I wanted to drop out for good, stay in Europe, write novels. They wanted me to get a degree. Finally I agreed (I think I was more scared than they were of my unreal plan), as long as I was spared the dreaded dorm. I needed a dailiness that included buying string beans; I can still hear the fervency with which I pleaded for the privilege of buying string beans. Such parents. My beautiful dead parents. Did they believe in the inspirational power of riboflavin? Perhaps not. But they believed in me. They paid the rent on a triangular walkup near Sheridan Square, a true pad, and I kept my part of the bargain, working hard and writing well enough to attract the attention of Professor X.

Just now I Googled him and discovered, to my pleased astonishment, he is still alive. Can it be that for all his dear paunchiness, heavy tread, nicotine-stained eyes, and sacred weariness, he was younger than I am as I write these words? What of his wife, whom I met at a tea when I was merely his student? I can still perfectly see her honest gray hair, angled in a becoming plane from a part on the right, stopping crisply just above her shoulders. Dear Frau Professor X. I hope she is still on earth and healthy, allowed to keep her hair. I hope she has a young lover who drives a sports car and brings her unspeakable pleasure.

In the sixties, a feminist mantra held that sisters didn't fuck other women's husbands or lovers. Exceptions might be made if you were all in it together, as long as the sponsoring fantasy rose well and truly out of the ladies' libidos, and you (we) weren't just indulging the guy. Now comes *Big Love* to the little screen, and *tout* America is talking about sister-wives. It's different, oh yes, if you have a woman's blessing to frolic with her mate—and God's smile to boot. But it's not apples and oranges. Apples and pomegranates, maybe.

In the good affair, the mistress never forgets that the husband/lover is hers on loan. She knows she must send him home to his wife better than she received him, like a borrowed car returned washed and waxed and brimming with high-test gas.

No lipstick-smudges on his collar. No diseases. Please, please don't get pregnant. Nix on the 4 A.M. phone calls to his home, even if crazy desperate. Be thoughtful about money—it's his wife's money, too. Don't be nonstop terrific: That's unfair competition with the woman who shares his laundry hamper.

It's not just that the righteous mistress wants to protect her lover. She cares about his wife. The wife isn't the enemy, merely the woman who got there first. The mistress doesn't misread the husband/lover's presence in her life. She knows no marriage is adultery-proof. People cheat on mates they adore. Sex at home may be terrific for both the participants, and one or both of them may want more or different. Generosity, not jealousy, is the barometer of love in a good affair. Reality is the umbrella.

"Keeping to one woman is a small price for so much as seeing one woman," G. K. Chesterton wrote in *Orthodoxy*. A poetic sentiment; but those who don't share his belief in a heavenly accountant may find the math flawed. Why does gratitude for one thing demand renunciation of another? Vegetarians wax pious about the bounty of the earth, but omnivores exemplify true reverence for the muchness. And I am best loved by a man who loves more, not fewer, women because he loves me.

A journalist pal called a few years back to say he was writing an article on how to tell when your marriage is in trouble. "When you're too unhappy to have an affair," I offered.

Professor X, a good writer and decent man who later made the mistake of hitting on freshmen, took seriously the responsibility of being my first married man. He made sure I understood how much he loved his wife and his marriage. He let me know the limits. (I had limits of my own, but that's another story.) We had maybe a dozen meetings, never public, and then, just somehow, we were over. A talky last tryst, without sex, and he grandly gave me a first edition of his second novel, inscription so layered and coded a lawyer might have composed it. His clear priorities set the standard. Nothing turned me off more surely in the years to come than the sordid plaint at the bar: "My wife doesn't understand me."

In a long-term affair, one that is grand as well as good, there are two triangles. As the mistress is the shadow other woman in relation to the marriage, the wife is the other woman to the illicit couple—their vulnerable girl-child. Like a sleeping infant snuggled between her parents in the nuptial bed on a Sunday morning, the wife dreams she is safe, and the dream must come true.

The adulterers know that protecting the wife's innocence is the non-negotiable price tag on the pleasure they share. And in affectionately colluding to that end, they fulfill a procreative and nurturing urge they must otherwise squelch.

Married Man to Mistress: "It would kill her to know."

Mistress: "Dearest, she isn't going to know."

MM: "I'll never leave her. I can't live without you, but I'll never leave her."

M: "I don't want you to leave her."

MM: "I know it's unfair to you—"

M: "It's perfectly fair. I have what I want of you."

MM: "I'm the luckiest man in the world."

M: "That's how I want you to feel. We're all lucky. Kiss me."

Several months ago, the editor of this anthology sent an e-mail containing two sentences: "Warner has requested that all events revealed in your memoirs be accurate. (This book will be essays only, no fiction.)" The cautionary editorial note came in the wake of the James Frey kafuffle and doubtless reflects a prevailing anxiety in publishing, but it had irony writ all over it. Mistresses are liars in the protection of their secret lives, and good liars; they have had to get over the notion that being a lousy liar is a virtue. Even an ex-mistress describing a lover some half-century ago may fudge the physical description and other revealing details. Professor X is not his name. The purported conversation above may or may not have taken place.

The British novelist John Fowles wrote that the real infidelity is the lie to cover the infidelity. He was right, and he was wrong.

In my early thirties, I did a stupid thing: I momentarily made a religion out of honesty and openness and insisted that my beloved MM, the fifth and final such successor to Professor X, tell his wonderful wife about me and then meet my parents. I thought our lies insulted and patronized them. I thought we could teach the world about sharing. My highly moral and ethical father was fond of saying that the blunt truth can be a blunt weapon; and, oh, how I bludgeoned people by coming out. My amour's wife carried on with her usual grace; my parents eventually recovered; but you can't create a Bohemian frolic by fiat; no way did I add to the sum of happiness in the world.

Sometimes doing unto others as you would have them do unto you is just another name for having your head up your ass.

I didn't recant, and I won't, but I moved on. I got out of the mistress business. I married twice, for love—real and human love, and gave birth to a daughter and then a son. With all respect to Justice Douglas, and with the most tender regard for MM, it was a far, far better thing I did.

Mistress, wife, or lover, my wiring makes it possible and desirable for me to live so no man has to lie to me. "Bring her home, I'll make breakfast in the morning." There's my comfort level, my notion of how to be honored. But it's not everyone's definition of keeping the faith. There are superb, strong women who just don't want to know. Unkindness is the real infidelity.

The other woman has to respect the *other* other woman's otherness. The wife is the mistress's mother, sister, daughter, and above all else she is herself, her absolute singular precious self. How lucky to have her in one's life. Loving her husband is a small price to pay for so much as knowing her name.

PHANTOM WIFE

▼

Victoria Zackheim

I was fighting the flu, but decided to stop by a friend's dinner party on my way home from the airport. There were five diners seated at the table and an empty chair. The hostess introduced me to her guests. One I knew, a charming woman who entertained with sharp British humor and an easy laugh. She was accompanied by a man I found very attractive, with intelligent eyes and one of those faces you immediately trust. He was from Northern Ireland; his accent was lovely.

I took the empty chair to the Irishman's right and joined in the conversation. It took little time to recognize that he and I were the only non-drinkers; the others were into their fourth bottle of wine.

As the minutes progressed, so, too, did my flu symptoms. I fought to ignore them because I found this man intriguing and seductive. We started with the usual small talk and quickly segued into his life, his past. I remember his story unfolding and my resolve to listen calmly, dis-passionately, although this drama was among the most impassioned I had ever heard. It was about Northern Ireland, taking American citizenship, a nine-month prison detention for IRA activities that were never proven. It was about witnessing brutality and dehumanization and how, after an unexplained release by the judge, there was a whis-pered caution to leave the country before morning. In the thirty minutes we sat together, he divulged a history that struck me as something out of Kafka. "I'm shocked to be telling you this," he said. "I haven't discussed this for more than twenty years."

While my body temperature continued to rise and the voice in my head begged me to leave, I could not move; I was mesmerized by this stranger, leaning close and speaking in a low, lilting voice. Fever gave way to chills and I made to leave. "Could you walk me to my car?" I asked, explaining that the streetlight was out and I was parked in a space blanketed in darkness. He agreed, we excused ourselves and left.

We stood at my car and continued talking. It had been years since my last relationship and I was fidgety and unsure. I was also about to lose my meal. My reaction to him was so strong that, when he explained that his dinner companion was an old college friend and not a date, I felt a rush of relief. Standing there, we discovered a shared love of opera, the sea, and traveling. I found myself searching for reasons not to be attracted. After all, if he was so wonderful, what were my chances? After forty minutes, we heard the others walking toward their cars and I did something I had never done: jotted my number on a scrap of paper, tucked it into his hand, and asked him to call. When I drove away, it was with a pounding headache tinged with expectation.

Several days later, a date was made and he arrived at my door. Dressed up and ready for the opera, there was electricity between us. We sat in a local bistro and talked about work and family. I learned that he had been divorced for many years and had not seen his wife, children, or grandchildren for most of them. They lived nearby, but there had been a rift—he wasn't even sure what had caused it—and all contact had been severed. I urged him to do whatever was necessary to reconnect and he told me that years of attempts had discouraged him. I was so attentive to the conversation that I dropped a large spoonful of pasta sauce on my silk blouse. When I patted it away and wiped at the spot with a damp linen napkin, the silk clung to my breasts like the material in a wet-T-shirt competition. He graciously averted his eyes and I nearly fell in love.

The opera was *La Bohème* and we both cried. It was the first of many operas we would attend in San Francisco, New York, Paris. Over the next month we took walks, met for dinner, had lengthy telephone conversations, and exchanged frequent e-mails. There were a few conversations about his wife and children. "I can't believe I'm talking about this," he told me several times. When I questioned why, he reminded me that he was a very private man. I wondered if this was his upbringing or the result of nine months of prison interrogation.

The time finally came for The Next Move. I assumed that he shared my excitement and anticipation, but I soon learned that we were in very different places. "I've only been in love once," he told me. "I'm not sure I can fall in love again." My smile communicated "Gee, who said anything about falling in love?" but love was certainly on my mind as we ascended the staircase to my bedroom. Conscious of my voluptuous body (read: overweight), I kept all lights extinguished. Since I knew absolutely nothing about the art of seduction, there were no candles, no rosebuds strewn across the bed. I hadn't daubed on perfume for thirty years! Was it like they said, like riding a bicycle? This was far more enjoyable than any bike ride. My new friend was a cuddler, thoughtful and determined to please. After we made love, we fell into a long and pleasurable sleep. (Did I remember that the cleaning crew was arriving early the next morning—and they had a key? When the boss passed me on the staircase and whispered "Busted!" I flinched, nearly cried from embarrassment, considered throwing myself in front of the next train . . . and then I giggled.)

Over the many weekends that followed, I became aware of something unsettling that I could not identify. There was adoration on his face, yet adoring words were rarely uttered. I was certain he wasn't seeing another woman, yet he held back. Why couldn't he just let go? As the months passed, I began to feel that we were never alone, that something hovered over us, as if we were marionettes and an unseen puppeteer was controlling the strings. One day, I finally understood: All around us was the muted presence of his former wife, the only woman he had ever loved.

We lived our lives apart during the week, which allowed us to work without interruption, and then we were together every weekend and through many trips abroad. I continued to be seduced by his Belfast accent, his left-wing politics, and his curious mind; by his cynical attitude toward religion and his skewed view of human nature, which included a general distrust of all forms of government. I had never been with a man who was so attentive, so loving and tender, or who was so supportive of my work and my life. From 600-count sheets to recognizing when I needed cheering, he was there. Not a romantic—never flowers or frills—but loving and good.

Near the end of our first year together, he asked me to sit down, there was something he wanted to say. "I'm happier, more joyful, than I've been since I was a child," he told me. "Even my brothers and sisters comment on it. They say you're the best thing that's ever happened to me, and they're right."

My heart soared! I was about to become the princess who found her prince.

"However," he continued, his face becoming somber. In that *however* I heard doom, a diagnosis of cancer, an admission of having someone else, someone who shared his bed during the week. "I think we should stop seeing each other. You deserve to meet someone capable of making a commitment, which I can't do."

I was stunned. How could being happy together be bad? I wanted to cry and plead. Instead, I explained that I was satisfied with our arrangement and that if I ever wanted more—living together, marriage—I would let him know. Until then, why go our separate ways? I marveled at the steadiness of my voice, the logic of my argument, my ability to push aside that lived-happily-forever-after part that triggered panic. I could not admit that I had already entered that fantasizing stage—sharing a home, filling it with friends and families—for fear he would walk out. I loved him, was happy for the first time in years. Revealing my dreams would bring this to an end. If a relationship is a song, then I chose to listen to the music, not the words.

This same conversation was repeated every year for the next six years. "I'm not sure I can make the commitment you want, that you deserve." Each time I felt that hovering presence, the phantom wife, the woman who had excised this man from her life and the lives of their children, yet remained a quotidian presence. More than a presence: she held a grip on his heart. It troubled me that I understood something he could not: that despite his anger toward her, he was unable—perhaps would never be able—to disengage from their sacred bonds of marriage. The phantom wife, the other woman, followed us to the opera, to Europe; she floated above our bed and was occasionally joined by his entire family and the Catholic Church. Despite eschewing religion, he was an Irish Catholic who had attended Catholic schools, where he was reminded daily that divorce was a sin in the eyes of God and community.

In time, I became part of his family—there were ten siblings still living, fifty nieces and nephews, most of them scattered around northern California and Belfast—and he became part of mine. My children were delighted to see me so happy and they made a place for him in their families. When my daughter gave birth to twin girls, he rushed teary-eyed to the hospital. His excitement was so poignant for me, knowing that all the while he was thinking of the grandchildren he had never seen, would not recognize if they passed him on the street.

As our relationship flourished, I encouraged him to talk about the disconnection from his ex-wife and children. He related stories about his wife, how time had driven a block of ice between them. "The last ten years of marriage," he told me. "I forgot what it was to laugh and be joyful." I did my best to be witty, engaging. If laughter and joy were what he sought, I'd make it happen.

It was New Year's Eve day and I was putting together my outfit for the evening. We were meeting friends for dinner and then wandering wherever the desire took us. Perhaps the gala being offered by the San Francisco Symphony or a walk along the Embarcadero. The phone rang and I answered "Happy New Year!" I heard his voice, how it was flat, constricted. I became alarmed. "Is everything okay?" After six years, I knew to discern that subtle shift in tone.

"You won't believe who just called."

I didn't have to ask. It had been eleven years since he had seen his ex-wife, yet I was certain it was she. Their daughter was ill, there was a crisis, the wife could no longer handle it alone and needed his help. What did I think? I thought it was an opened door and that he should step through. Perhaps this was the break we had hoped for, the chance to put faces on the names of all of those grandchildren never seen. "She wants to come over in an hour and talk." I told him to meet with her, listen to what she had to say. If she wanted to talk until midnight, that was fine. I did not add that my heart was pounding, that nausea was welling up and I had to control the urge to vomit.

I took a hot bath, trimmed my nails, tried on several outfits, as if expecting him to arrive. Everywhere I went, the phone was in my hand. He called at six to say they were still talking. I e-mailed a friend, revealed the drama unfolding, and we commiserated. What were they doing? Talking? Kissing? Laughing about what a fool I had been to think he would stay with me? He checked in at nine, again at eleven, finally at two in the morning. Yes, they were talking and he was learning the depth of her anger. He called at eight in the morning to say they were again in conversation, again at ten to repeat her phrases of anger. I heard a sound of protest and footsteps rushing away, staccato receding across the hardwood floor. There was no need to be there; I understood the rage that can pass between two people who once shared dreams, family, love.

How could a man be shut off from his family for eleven years? Anger suffered by a wife and passed on to her children; accusations real or imagined, some tragic, others banal, that easily twist and distort into a lie that becomes someone's truth. Old pain, grievances, and suffering, heartache resurrected and exposed in a dreadful arrangement of words. On this first day of the year: shared confusion; intense emotion; denouement.

I waited for him, the supportive, loving girlfriend, but I felt shut out. They were sharing anger, such an intimate emotion, perhaps more intimate than sex. I ate everything in sight and tried to get lost in a novel, but found myself reading the same passage over and over. He had never expressed anger toward me, yet he was communicating this to his ex-wife. Should I be worried?

After the new year, our lives returned to normal. The only difference was that he was having occasional phone discussions with her. I encouraged this, encouraged anything that would give him back his family. When he told me he was flying to Arizona to assist his daughter, I helped him book his flight and hotel room, said all the supportive and loving things I sincerely felt. "Do you want me to come along?" I asked, but he said no. And then he mentioned that his ex-wife would be there and I instantly wondered if they were sharing a room.

He spent four days with his daughter and let her know that he was there for her, that he had always been there. He returned with photographs of beautiful children and their beaming, joyful grandfather. He talked about them, went into lengthy descriptions of each one, and emanated the joy I had waited years to see.

During the weekdays, when we were apart, I vacillated between delight for this reconnection and the fear that he would choose them over me. I had renewed fantasies of selling our homes and buying a large house on a hill, with many bedrooms for his enormous family. We would sit at either end of a long refectory table and revel in the joys of having our brothers and sisters, children and grandchildren seated between us.

It was a year after this reconciliation that we returned to France and Ireland. By this time, my French friends knew and loved him, his Irish family knew and loved me. Our visit with friends in the south of France was easy and intimate, with long walks and leisurely dinners on the terrace overlooking acres of vineyards. When we set off in the car, I was the driver, he was the co-pilot, and we wove our way into the Gaillac region, through villages and valleys leading to the airport, sharing ideas on purchasing a farmhouse, perhaps an old *moulin*, and entertaining our extended family. We stopped along the way, photographed hillsides where we could easily live, shared all the excitement of young lovers planning a future.

Ireland was not France. There were no leisure moments, no sauntering. Instead, we raced through the south—he drove and I held on tightly, our little car zooming along narrow roads turned into paved canyons by the towering hedges running alongside. He was confident of being able to stop if a lorry suddenly appeared, but I doubted the mechanics. After one day I was exhausted and tense, wishing to be anywhere but in that little bullet-car. I had been to Ireland many times, although never to the southwest coast, so my list of places to visit consisted of three or four; the list of places he wanted me to see went on for pages. I explained that the castles, cliffs, and vistas would be there for the next trip and I was not interested in visiting yet another manor of Lord Someone. "No matter what I do," he shot back, "I can't make you happy."

I chewed on that and then recalled that this was exactly the same phrasing he had used when describing a vacation he had taken with his wife. No matter what he did, he could not make her happy. I mentioned this and his brow furrowed. "Perhaps your definition of 'happy' was not hers," I suggested. "Perhaps *you* decided what would make her happy and then you set out to achieve that . . . without consulting her." This was not the first time I had pointed out that she was being blamed for a problem that might have emanated from him and it certainly was not something he wanted to hear. He argued my analysis, but I could see that he was listening carefully.

It was the weekend before our sixth Valentine's Day together and we were about to leave for a long walk. Instead, he sat down. "I need to talk to you," he said. I sat and waited, phrases running through my mind to assuage his guilt, convince him that this lifestyle together could go on indefinitely. He removed a letter from his pocket and began to read. His voice was quavering and I wanted to snatch it from his hands. "Just tell me," I said. Intense heat rose from my neck and I had a sudden sense that I was falling.

As he read, I recognized the words. "I've never been as joyful as I am with you. Everyone who knows me believes that you're the best thing that's ever happened in my life, and I agree." If so, why this tightness in my chest? Daubing at his tears, he read, "I can't make the commitment you want. Therefore, I'm ending our relationship."

I wanted to argue with him, but there were no words.

I reached out for the letter, but he folded it carefully and slipped it back into his pocket. That simple gesture said it all: no discussion. Without a word, I walked upstairs and dropped his clothing and books, his computer equipment and opera glasses, into a suitcase. He stood behind me, offering to come back later for his things. "Oh no," I explained. "When you leave, there is no coming back." I wept and then we walked to his car, the suitcase bumping over the road. We kissed good-bye and he drove away.

He called several times over the next week, said that I was his dearest friend, the person he trusted most in the world. Could we get together every week for a movie or dinner? "Absolutely not," I told him, knowing that each meeting would result in my pleas, my desperate attempts to change his mind. Pride goeth before the fall? Not always. Sometimes, pride after the fall is one's only protection: I'd been through that humiliation before and would never go back.

Months later he e-mailed about an investment we shared. I informed him that my mother had fallen and broken her back; he asked if he could visit her. We met at my mother's and I invited him to come along to an author's reading. In the car, I heard the same stories, the same problems, of a man stuck in his past. I found myself checking my watch. He was still the man I had loved, kind and caring, but he was no longer beguiling.

That meeting was more than three years ago.

The last I heard, he was living with his ex-wife.

THE MAN WITH THE BIG HANDS

▼

Maxinne Rhea Leighton

The man with the big hands was the youngest of four children. The only American-born son of an immigrant family who had escaped the pogroms in Eastern Europe, his birth was seen as a miracle, a bridge from the old world to the new. Unlike his siblings, who married into the roots of their ancestry, the youngest one chose a woman with foxy red hair, long, perfectly manicured nails, and credit cards that did not include Lane Bryant. Her family owned a home in Westchester.

They met at my parents' wedding. Three dances and a short time later, they were married. The bride's dress was not borrowed and the groom's tuxedo not rented. My mother said they had a beautiful honeymoon in a Florida resort. My parents celebrated theirs at a run-down hotel in the Catskills. My mom never got to Florida. That was her dream. In Big Hands and Thin Red's wedding

photographs, they looked as perfect as the two plastic fig-
urines on the top of their wedding cake. Theirs was to be
a childless union.

I was born of parents decades older than they. Big
Hands and Thin Red became my idealized mom and dad.
Big Hands was energetic and the only man in the family
who resembled a modern person. He was a renegade type
and moved faster than my father and just about everyone
else. Red was larger than life in her cashmere sweaters,
pencil-thin skirts, patent leather high-heel shoes, large diamond ring, and a well-made-up face that included Chanel-
red lipstick. A non-filtered Camel cigarette often rested
between her fingers. In a family of women who wore oversized clothing with flowered prints, she became a movie
star and they called her Maureen, after the actress with
the last name of O'Hara. I called her Red.

Of all the children in the family, I was the only one
with red hair. Surrounded by brunettes and dyed blondes,
when I looked at Red, I felt connected in a way that was
unique to what I saw around me. We were linked by color
and I wanted to be just like her.

When my parents worked past midnight, which was
often, I spent the night at Grandma's apartment right
above our store, which was a luncheonette and soda foun-
tain that served sandwiches and sold toys. Dolls, trucks,
and games lined the display cabinets. There were metal
racks with comic books that my mother said I couldn't
read. I was surrounded by a world that other children

could only dream of, yet I was never allowed to take things off the shelf and play with them.

Big Hands worked alongside my father, but worked fewer hours. My father rarely got home until after the late evening news. While he closed up every night and spent two hours on the subway and bus to get to our home in the Coney Island housing projects, Big Hands drove to his middle-class Italian neighborhood in his DeSoto Adventurer. My mother often said that the biggest mistake of her life was introducing Thin Red to Big Hands. One time I asked her why and she said he had only married her for her money.

On weekends, when I was little, my mother worked alongside my father and Big Hands. When I was older, she worked full time. Saturday was the busiest day of the week and the only evening they sometimes stayed open until midnight. Red often "helped out," serving tuna fish sandwiches, ice cream, and milk shakes at the counter with the worn red leather stools. She always wore a perfectly pressed starched cotton smock so she wouldn't get dirty.

During the late nights, I slept in my grandmother's apartment above the store. At bedtime, my mother tucked me in and went back downstairs to work. Then Red would come up and read me books with colorful pictures. Sometimes, Big Hands joined her and sat on the side of the bed and listened. I was happy with them.

But one day, Big Hands changed. Warm hugs were replaced with clutching movements that made his fingers seem sharper, his arms longer, his hands wider. It didn't matter what he touched—a shaker of salt, a ten-dollar bill out of the cash register, or a doll off the shelf—his movements were fragmented and erratic. He seemed cold. I remember thinking I must have done something to make him angry. So I smiled more and tried to be a good girl.

Then there was the Christmas of the Betsy Wetsy doll. I don't remember how late they worked that night, but it was almost daylight when I heard footsteps near my bed. It was my parents, Big Hands, and Red. They had a box covered with shiny wrapping paper and were placing it beside me. When they saw that I was awake, they turned on the light and Red and my mom helped me unwrap it. Inside was the one thing I wanted more than anything in the world: a curly-haired doll with blue eyes and red pursed lips that I could feed. She wet her pants like a real baby. But as Betsy was placed in my arms, Red glanced down at the doll and then shrieked. "How could you do that?" she wailed at Big Hands. "You gave her a sick doll."

Whatever Red saw, my mother saw too and she cried hysterically. "Look at her—the eyes are crossed!"

Big Hands defended himself. "A customer brought the doll back. It's Christmas Eve. What else could I do but give him the one we saved for Maxinne. She's a baby. She'll never know the difference."

"You are a schnorrer," my mother screeched repeatedly, using the Yiddish word for a cheat or a parasite who takes from others as if it were his own. Throughout all of this, my father sat silent in a wooden chair, the one with the shaky leg that Grandma kept in the corner.

Big Hands began visiting me. I wasn't sure I was the one he was actually looking for when his shadow crossed the darkened bedroom at my grandmother's, until his hands, his big hands, found me. At first he touched me comfortingly, rocking me to sleep in his arms. Then the touch became a kiss on the cheek, the forehead, and then the lips. Hands on my shoulders moved to my flat, six-year-old chest and down further to my vagina. That first night, when Big Hands began to rub me and himself, I heard my grandmother's snoring in the next room. I listened closely, rather than focus on that long thing that began to grow in his hand. "Want to lick? Come on, little one, just like a Tootsie, Tootsie Roll lollipop." As it moved toward my mouth, I saw it was much bigger than a lolly and did not have a white stick at the end of it. His "lolly" went into my mouth, up and down, repeatedly—liquid, wet—big hands moving quickly, holding on to my tiny shoulders. I tried to scream. I wanted to run, but I had no legs. I stared ahead like Betsy Wetsy, with her eyes going in two different directions. Then I would not have to look at him. I wet the bed.

"It's our secret," he said.

"Where's Grandma?" I asked, crying. He stopped me with his wet finger on my lips. Red and Mommy were working downstairs.

"If you tell secrets, no one is going to love you anymore."

Two had become three: Big Hands, Red, and me. I became the other woman at six.

As I got older, he would rub his penis up against me every time he passed behind the counter to get to the cash register. The night visits had dropped away. I told my mother, not about the nights upstairs at Grandma's, but about this. How it terrified me.

"Everyone is frightened of Big Hands," she said. "I can't stand him. But Red loves you like her own child. They have the money to send you to college. Ignore it."

I spent less time behind the counter.

Red and I talked on the phone a lot. I would lie on my bed at home, talking on my blue desktop princess line. Big Hands would arrive at some point in our conversation, pick up the extension in their bedroom, and ask questions about my love life. Red would giggle like a girl and tell him to stop embarrassing me, that I was too young to have a boyfriend.

When my best friend Dara's boyfriend came on to me, he said it would be our secret. He grabbed me by the waist and we kissed. I pushed his body away and ran. I could not believe this was happening. The next time I saw them together, I pretended it never did. Dara was slimming down on WeightWatchers, but I had begun to stuff my face. "You're getting fat like your mother," Big Hands said. I grew to hate my own body rather than him. Then I stopped eating and lost a huge amount of weight in a short period of time. My mother dragged me to doctors and tea-leaf readers. The tea-leaf readers said I had a curse on me. Red said, "I'll get you to eat, I'll get you to eat." She made American food and homemade black-out cake. I wanted her to love me.

Frequently, we ate together at her house and Big Hands would arrive late. When he appeared, I would excuse myself and go to the bathroom. "Get out of me, get out of me," I begged, sticking my fingers down my throat, bringing up what I had ingested with Red but could not hold down when he was around. They drove me home after these dinners. But one night, Red said that Big Hands would drive me home alone. It was a long drive from their house to mine.

"I've started meeting with counselors at school and talking about colleges. I really want to go to Emerson in Boston," I told him.

"How are you going to pay for that, young lady?" he asked.

"I'll apply for loans and a scholarship."

"We are going to pay," he said.

My mother was right! When I finished writing my college applications, I called him from a phone booth. "I'm going to need the money for the fees. When can I get that from you?" I wanted to know.

"I never said I was going to pay for school."

"You promised."

"No, I didn't."

I slammed down the phone. He told my mother and Red that I had made it all up, that he never said he would.

I thought Red would say, "Of course we'll pay." She knew my parents could not. She said nothing.

That year, instead of paying for my college, Big Hands and Red gave large donations to the synagogue. He was heralded as an honorable man and was always asked up to the Torah for the aliyah, read on Saturday mornings in synagogue, an honor and a blessing in Jewish tradition. My father never missed a minyan, the daily morning prayers requiring ten men. In fact, they never made a minyan without him. Unlike Big Hands, he could not contribute large sums of money and he rarely received any recognition. I lost faith in a religious institution that could reward a man based not on his deeds, but his wallet, until my father said to me that a relationship with God was a very personal thing, one on one; that it was not a triangle, but a straight line between two parties.

I went to a college close to home for one year. Then, with financial aid and scholarships, I got into a school in upstate New York. While it was not the school I had dreamed of in Boston, it was for me the beginning of a new life. Red and Big Hands drove me and my parents up to school for orientation. They were the only ones in the family with a car.

Beginning life away from home did not change that I remained the other woman. I dated men where I was the other woman to their mother, ex-girlfriend, job, pet. I wanted a monogamous, non-secretive, committed relationship, yet I remained a minor league player rather than a major league pitcher. If not for a relationship I had years later with a man I called the Professor, I never would have confronted Big Hands.

For the first six months of our relationship, I ignored the fact that the Professor and I never spent an entire night together. Weekends were off limits. When I finally questioned him and he admitted he was married, I sobbed the way I had done so often at night, after Big Hands left me to go back downstairs. When the professor and his wife separated and he was suddenly available, I still remained a secret. Finally, I broke it off.

Big Hands had just had a heart attack. I called before I went to the hospital and spoke to Red. We didn't talk much anymore. She focused her energy on new babies born into the family. When I walked into the hospital room, I recognized the red hair, though it had faded to an orange hue. She was no longer thin and the makeup, once glamorous, looked like a painted mask. She was bent over and shorter. I kissed her on the cheek and she was neither warm nor cold. When she kissed me back, her red Chanel lipstick left a mark on my cheek, as it had for decades. The diamond ring still sparkled on a spotted hand that had stopped holding non-filtered cigarettes decades earlier.

Big Hands was sitting in a chair, hooked up to monitors. I brought a chair up to him, so close that our knees almost touched. I spoke in a whisper. Red stared out the window as we spoke. "Why did you hurt me?" I asked. "Why did you do what you did to me?" Part of me wanted to get an answer before he died; the other hoped the question would strike him dead in my presence. He placed his hands on his balls and scratched them throughout the conversation. This was the man with whom all secrets began. It was with him that I became the other woman at the age of six.

"I had a cat, Maxinne, I loved that cat. Your father forgot to light the stove in the back of the store. It was in the middle of winter. The cat froze to death. He killed my cat. I was just a little boy. Then, when I was older, I went to borrow money to buy some property. I wanted to be in real estate, not in the store. I hated that store. Your dad found out and told our mother and she made the developer give me back all that I had borrowed." (Borrowing money and owing anyone anything was a *shandeh*, a shame.) "After that," he continued, "no one in the neighborhood would give me a loan. I was stuck in the store forever. Your father stole my life. So I took the one thing that meant more to him than life itself: you. I stole you and what I took you'll never get back. I killed what your father loves most."

With the exception of a few select cousins, one of whom I called String Bean, I became estranged from my family. String Bean was the only other person in my family whose rage and hurt toward Big Hands matched my own. Long ago, Big Hands hadn't stood up for String Bean's father when he should have. He'd chosen money instead.

Recently, String Bean invited me to meet his newest granddaughter, Tomasina. As I walked into their home, I was amazed to find my cousin holding a child with a halo of red hair. Tomasina looked at me with her beautiful blue eyes, transfixed on my red mane. As I held her in my arms, supporting her back with the gentleness of my embrace, she looked at me as if she knew me.

"This is what Maxinne looked like when she was born," String Bean informed everyone in the room. "The only one in the family with red hair. She is the only one like you," he told his granddaughter. "Look how she's watching you." He smiled.

Tomasina continued staring at my hair. This little redhead was born into a family lineage where our uniqueness had made us visible. Her beauty and joyful eyes seemed like a familiar scenario from long ago, before I knew that dolls had crossed eyes and men who cast shadows had ill intentions.

"A kindred spirit," they all pronounced.

As I held her, waves of foreboding moved through my body. She empathically sensed my fear and began to cry. Would this little red-haired child have my fate? I felt fear take hold and passed her back to her grandfather's arms.

I looked around the living room. It was clear that there were no triangles here. As I observed String Bean with Tomasina, I saw in his eyes—and those of everyone else in the room—how much this child was cherished. After all these years, I could almost feel that for myself.

A HAND ON THE NECK

▼

Laurie Stone

At a lonely time in my life, I walked up and down Broadway looking at couples. I watched a man place his hand at the back of a woman's neck and steer her along, his fingers curving lightly toward her throat, a gesture that could have looked overbearing but to me looked sexy. What struck me was his access to her body.

The man who touched me that way was Jed.* I liked it, even when I didn't like him. He was generous, but you had to let him run things. He'd swoop down on people, offering gifts and time, then freeze up if you asked for something he didn't want to give. Friends would drift away, girlfriends careen off like balloons with the air let out. He'd look into himself, like a kid dismantling a gadget, then sweep away

---

*Names, physical descriptions, places, and occupations have been changed to protect the privacy of the people described.

the pieces when a new woman was installed. I'd disappear, sometimes for a long time. Eventually, he'd call, and we'd meet. I liked a hand moving out of darkness. He'd describe a garden he was designing and fill me in on his kids. This one was fasting, that one passionately playing the violin. As we'd get up to leave the bar or café, his hand would move to my neck, pressing down a little and forward, and I'd think, *This is how he does it.*

Anger didn't discourage him. Silence did. We were alike in that way. I thought that if I'd been born a man with a mother who adored me, I could have become him.

Like Jed, I touched people without asking. I'd stand next to a woman at a party and realize my hand was moving up and down her back. She might not even be a friend. I touched the faces of people when they leaned in to kiss me, ruffled the hair of kids, traced the down on their arms.

I liked the temperature of Jed's hands. I liked that he didn't ask, though we weren't a good fit in bed. During our early years, I was jealous of his girlfriend, Robin, who was beautiful and kind. I was becoming friends with her, but in those days I didn't know how to be loyal to a woman. I looked at the world as a jungle, and I was often hurt.

One time, when I was unattached and Jed and Robin were taking a break from their relationship—though not officially split—I spent a weekend at his country house. I was in my early twenties. He was in his mid-thirties, already a star in his field. He made things beautiful: rooms, food, flower arrangements, women. He bought presents people didn't return: sweaters, scarves, perfume. When he started making money, he transformed a barn in upstate New York into a studio, planting flowers and vegetables out back, where his sheltie, Malone, chased squirrels. He cooked with herbs, uncorked pricey wine. There were irises and tulips on chests he'd unearthed in thrift shops and stripped down.

I could feel his unhappiness when I arrived. He was reading under a tree, and he hesitated before offering me an abrupt hug. He would have preferred, I think, to come upon me on a beach and push me down on a dune, have me fast and unfussy. But I was there.

We had dinner and afterward climbed onto his big bed, which was underneath a skylight, and we watched the stars and moon move across the sky. His comforter smelled of Robin's orange-water splash. Jed's drawings were off kilter on the walls. Malone jumped up and snuggled with us, burrowing his cold snout into my side. The domesticity of the scene coupled with the fakeness of our feelings made me feel like an intruder and made me want to have sex. Jed's body was muscular, though he ate too much to be sleek, and his manner was more shambling than smooth. He wasn't beautiful, but covered by plowing ahead. He had long reddish blond hair tied back in a ponytail, rimless glasses that etched marks beside his nose, and pale gray eyes that were hard to fathom and seemed, often, to be mocking. His allure arose from his truculence, success, and unavailability. Most of the time we were together we argued or laughed. He was good at telling stories, tagging characters with accents and tics. But that night, on his bed, our tongues were thick. It didn't occur to me he might have felt guilty toward Robin for cheating on her and toward me for not caring enough.

We'd fooled around before, once in his apartment, but it had been furtive and rushed and exciting for those reasons. Now, there was nothing to interrupt us. Jed asked for what he wanted and I was accommodating, as I more or less watched. If he noticed, he didn't seem disturbed. We made love several more times that weekend and it didn't get better. I remember lying beside him, sweaty and lonely, thinking his coldness meant I'd asked for it. Over the next few years, we had sporadic sex. I liked his reaching out. I liked knowing that, afterward, I wouldn't want more. As we'd part, trotting down the stairs of his apartment or riding the elevator down from mine, his hand would move to my neck, erasing thoughts I didn't want to be there.

Over the years, my friendship with Robin deepened, but I didn't tell her about Jed and me. I was afraid she'd hate me, even though they'd stopped speaking. One time, Jed and I talked about our gloomy weekend, and I said I'd been hurt. He acknowledged his remoteness, but by then fifteen or twenty years had passed and I didn't care about the reasons. Some people, in the way they let go of me, make me dislike myself. Jed didn't let go.

One night, when he was married to his third wife, Emily—they'd been together for about ten years—he intimated he wanted to spend the night. We'd had lobster and champagne, his treat. I wasn't seeing anyone, but I said no, saying I no longer slept with married men. It was true, though not the reason. I didn't want to be intimate with him. He was disappointed but didn't sulk. He didn't make that the thing, even though it was always there.

I reckoned that, for him, I was proof he'd once had the power to give women pain. Emily was a car that had been dinged so often she no longer cried out. I'd travel to their country house to see them and Jed's four kids, two with Emily. I liked her—the way I'd been attracted to Robin—and Emily resembled the young Robin with her optimistic eyes, flowing honey hair, and long, athletic legs. Jed had sold the barn and built a compound beside a lake. Emily liked when I took Jed off her hands. He was happy to instruct his kids about music, astronomy, gardening, and food. He was interested in his children, but he didn't consider their care his job. He'd go off to his studio, far from the main house, returning for meals. When I was there, we'd canoe to a little island and he'd knead the knots in my back.

During one of those visits, I arrived in a sorry state, in flight from a failing romance. There was another guest there, Luc, a French musician Emily was writing songs with. He was hot for her and younger than Jed, though older than Emily, who had a thing for guys who'd packed on the years. She liked stability, after growing up with hippie parents who did so many drugs they had barely held on to their academic jobs. Now, as she put it, it was her turn to rebel.

Luc and I helped her with the kids and housework. The more carefree we acted, the more morose Jed grew. I thought I should be loyal to him. I was eating his food, drinking his wine, sleeping on his sheets. But I was rooting for Luc, with his tight abs and lilting accent. I wanted Emily to rise up. We'd take the kids hiking and biking and tumble into the house, noisy and askew. Jed would glare at Luc and me as if we were kidnappers, and he'd badger Emily about things she'd left undone. On top of that, the stock market was tanking and design commissions were slowing. Jed's hair was thinning, his joints creaking, his paunch expanding. I'd watched him juggle girlfriends and wives for so many years. I liked seeing him squirm.

My last night there, ticked off by something incalculable, he shoved his chair out from the table before dessert and stomped off to his study. We hadn't spent time alone. When I'd first arrived and slunk out of my car, strained and weepy, his eyes had glazed over. He couldn't understand why I didn't have a family, success, money, a better boyfriend. I didn't know, either. That morning, I'd said I wanted to catch up and he'd nodded moodily, looking out at a cluster of pines. When night came, everyone went to bed except Jed and me. I read in the den while he worked. After midnight, he emerged looking rumpled, a deep crease between his eyes. He headed to the kitchen. I padded behind, calling his name. He turned, and we faced each other in the hall.

An antique table with gladiolas was against one wall. A yellow truck was underneath it, and inside the truck was a squeak toy belonging to Jed's current sheltie, Murphy. A tang of sweat rose off his shirt, which was frayed at the elbows, and there was grease on his khakis from buttered corn.

"Can we talk?" I asked, not knowing what I wanted. Maybe to be forgiven for siding with Luc or to soften the roughness around us. A dark look came into his eyes, and before I could understand what was happening, his hands were on my arms, squeezing hard. He shook me back and forth, as if he wanted to throw me against a wall. His mouth twisted, as he tried to rid himself of the intensity that swirled around us and that we didn't have a name for. It just arrived, invited by the strangest things. It kept puzzling us, as if the questions it prompted that could not be answered were part of its hook. The force of his hands fascinated and jammed me. I didn't speak.

"Not now," he hissed, "I told you I had a deadline." His eyes skittered from the clock to me, then back to the clock. "You ask for things I don't want to give."

I had an image of myself scratching at a screen door, a ghost or a raccoon. Someone else would not have waited up.

Emily had confided the way he sometimes hurled things and grabbed her. He was being more intimate than ever before, I supposed, but I didn't know what to do with it. All the years we'd known each other, what did we understand?

"Okay," I said, breaking free. He looked surprised, as if he didn't realize he was holding me that tight. I left him standing in the hall and in the morning I propped a note for Emily against a fruit bowl and drove off.

I expected a letter or an e-mail to arrive in a few days, saying he'd needed to blow off steam and was sorry. I told Emily about the incident and she laughed nervously. "You know how he gets, better than anyone."

"Actually, I don't. I've never seen him like that."

"He probably feels terrible, but you know how stubborn he is. He'll come around."

I wanted to say he could go fuck himself. I felt his hands on my skin, tasting something oily and sour. He'd crossed a line. A month later, he sent a letter but no apology. He said he was strained and surely I could understand. We both did things. It was no big deal. I didn't answer. A few months later he called and we talked. He didn't apologize. He said we were contentious types, two of a kind. He wanted to make a date, saying we could sort things out then. I said I needed to clear the air first and he ended the conversation.

Over the next few years he sent reminders that he was thinking of me. He'd tell me how I figured in a dream, as if the scenario was about me. He sent Christmas cards with pictures of his kids.

I didn't think I missed him, but I opened the notes hoping for an apology. Why couldn't I let it go? I didn't believe in avowals like *I love you* or *I will stay with you*. They should have included *I'm sorry*. I thought that under certain circumstances we could all turn icy or wild. Other people were allowed to slither in and out of my affections, even if I found them moral idiots or emotional defectives. But not Jed.

Four years almost to the day of our break, a letter arrived without a return address. The handwriting looked familiar. Jed was writing to say he'd dreamed of me again and was wondering why I was throwing away a friendship of thirty-five years for one misstep. I was pining about a different man and e-mailed Jed saying all he'd ever had to do was say he was sorry. He wrote that he thought he had. He didn't remember putting his hands on me or yelling. We e-mailed a few more times and he worried I'd demand a rehashing. I said it was okay.

I rode my bike to meet him along the river where the road is flat, pedaling fast, and I was damp by the time I arrived. He was waiting inside a café, tanned and slimmer, wearing rose-tinted glasses and a stud in one ear—the stylish bohemian getting on. He said that one of his kids was studying physics, another becoming a midwife. All were musical, one daughter was gay and had a girlfriend. Emily was producing a play, and he had a commission to design a botanic garden in Connecticut. There was a new dog, Tilda, and maybe Emily would bring her around. But a few hours passed and she didn't arrive, and Jed asked for the check before I wanted the evening to end.

I'd just returned from a week in Indiana, staying in a hotel room lined with mirrors. I'd recently become friends with a woman twenty years younger than I, tall and sexy, in her hair-tossing, mojo-working prime. The times we'd gone out, I'd watched men moth around her, their eyes becoming furred, and I'd felt myself become invisible. It was as if I were watching a storm churn up waves or an eagle swoop down to capture a field mouse, disquieting but inevitable.

Jed said I looked unchanged. I said it was yoga and some plastic surgery. But the thing was, he would have looked at me that way no matter what. I was nineteen when we met. I offered to split the check, but he waved me away. It was only a few paces from the table to the street, but before we were out the door, his hand was on my neck, pressing down, easing me forward. He kept it there while I unlocked the bike chain and placed it in my basket. He didn't let go until I was ready to ride off.

I could feel his hand as I rode to the river. A breeze was blowing, and the air smelled of high tide. I moved onto the bike path, which was lighted in places and in others dark. A mounted cop eased along. I smelled the horse, summer sweat and hay. Other bikers and runners streamed by. I rode past beach grass and the hulking ruins of decaying piers that were near where I'd lived when I was young. My apartment had had a fireplace. Jed would come by and we'd sit and watch the flames. I was poor and collected splintery crates to burn. The wood crackled and spit and sometimes made little whistling sounds like a sleeping animal, and it was like having someone doz-ing on your lap, a child or a man, a head lolling on your thighs. There were sizzling sounds and pops, a language that wasn't trying to express anything and that I preferred to words with their straining for exactness and disappoint-ing revelations.

I felt Jed's hand, forgetting its potential to turn treach-erous, forgetting that it didn't exist to hold or feed me, forgetting that it was just a hand with a life and will of its own. The knowledge wouldn't hold. I could feel it slipping all the time that the warmth of his fingers remained.

Seized

▼

Kathleen Archambeau

When I first met her at Trinity Place, I was seized. Struck by her beauty. Arrested by the clear streambed green eyes. Maybe it was the slight turn of her hips when she danced. Or the honest way she confessed to not having a very good time. When my arms first wrapped around her seafaring cotton ribbed sweater as we were leaving the bar, I was instantly taken.

Our next date started innocently enough, in the stinging light of the old San Francisco Museum of Modern Art. We stalked one another like jaguars, in the Italian architecture display. Later, we drove out to Fort Funston to watch the sun melt, sinking into the ocean, to a rim of India red. She sat close. Her slender thighs touched mine and the dance of pheromones flooded my limbs.

Some names have been changed out of respect for those involved.

We never ate dinner that night. We stole into a South of Market inn.

We took in one another's bodies. First, the nipple, soft as a tea rose; then, the inner thigh, white as whipped cream. Stunned into kissing the raspberry lips. Finally, finding the tangled gates to a world we would crack open for the next fourteen years. So natural, the fall into love.

Though our relationship started out in a collide of passions, it soon settled into a comfortable rhythm. I found out she didn't even like to dance. Most evenings were reserved for long conversations along Glen Park Canyon, where we took our German shepherd. There was talk of the new Expressionism art exhibit or the bisexual film at the Lumière; debates about where to get the best fish or organic vegetables; about the difference between taupe and beige or granite versus Corian. Long discussions about work and office politics, longer analyses of our friends' marriages and single lives. Often, we eschewed parties for the pleasure of one another's company.

She was diagnosed with seizure disorder seven years into our relationship, but medication controlled the seizures and we were happy together.

Fourteen years after we met, she spent the night in a Cosmos slur at a friend's house. I wasn't happy about it, but she was the spokesperson for her company's gay and lesbian employee group, so I figured she'd been carried away in the celebration of winning domestic partner benefits. The following Saturday morning, I awoke feeling cheerful. The day, however, did not start off well for her.

There was the unemptied dishwasher or the unfed dog—I can't remember which—but something put her in a bad mood. "Let's not fight," I said.

"We always fight," she told me.

This wasn't true, except for the last month or so. Since the seizures broke through. The neurosurgeon had been experimenting with a variety of drugs and we were hoping for the best.

I suggested a walk, a hike with the dog, a movie. "I don't want to go to a movie. We always go to movies," she said, and sulked back into the bedroom.

Unloading the dishwasher, I saw the curl of her butternut hair out of the corner of my eye. She went into the study and I followed.

"I have something to tell you," she said.

My heart fell to my feet, like an elevator skipping floors.

"I'm in love with someone else. I met her at work. I wasn't looking, it just happened."

"It doesn't just happen," I mustered.

"She's a bodybuilder, her name's Angie, you'd really like her," she said, adding that Angie had just left her lover. I told her I wouldn't and she said, "How can you say that? You don't even know her."

"This is what I know," I responded. "Angie started an affair while she was still living with another woman and while you were still living with me. She's breaking up a fourteen-year marriage with no concern for me or, for that matter, you. My guess is she lies and she cheats. I think I can safely say that she is not a nice person. I'm going to predict that she'll leave you just the way you're leaving me."

I ran into the bathroom of our Victorian cottage and locked the door. Between sobs, I dry-heaved into the toilet. She was banging on the door.

"Kathy, I didn't mean to hurt you. Come out, please!"

That night, we ripped into one another with an anger we'd never shown before. "You see this furniture?" I yelled. "You see this painting, this computer, this couch? You'll be leaving all of it!"

"I never wanted it!"

"That's what you say now, after I put you through school, got you a job at my old company, bought you all this stuff—"

"You can have the stuff! You're not as thin as you were when I met you—"

That caught me off guard; it entered under my skin like a sliver and would stay there long after this conversation ended.

Back and forth we went, each new sentence a blistering attack. She fell into a deep sleep midway through the night. I heated milk and honey, brandy and herbal tea, but failed to quiet the rage of thoughts.

The next morning, she promised she'd never see the woman again. Promised to change jobs, even though she had just been promoted and loved her work. She had thought about what we had together and didn't want to give that up. A crater formed in my stomach; I watched her as if I were observing a stranger.

One week of détente passed and then I found that I

no longer wanted to go home. I began acting erratically, staying with friends and not telling her where I was; going to hotels and calling late at night to let her know I wasn't coming home.

Two weeks later the seizures returned, petit mal seizures, up to four or five a day. We found ourselves seated across the desk from her Stanford neurosurgeon. It troubled me that she was still driving: a man having a seizure had just killed a family on the Golden Gate Bridge. When I asked the doctor if the seizures or the drugs could impair her driving, he said they could.

"You're trying to control me," she said, her face red and her pupils narrowed. "You're trying to take away my independence! I won't give up my driver's license." I tried to calm her, touched her forearm. "Don't touch me!" she nearly yelled.

"I just want to know if the seizures or the drugs could affect your judgment—"

The doctor rose. "I'll leave you two to work this out." He left the room.

One more week went by, now three weeks after she told me of the affair. She continued to take the new medication and her condition seemed stabilized. She called me at work to say she had changed her mind and wanted to go into couples counseling.

"You've already decided, haven't you?"

"Yes, I pretty much have." Her voice sounded like a safe door closing.

Her new lover, Angie, was as unaccomplished as

I was successful. The two of them came from different worlds: country club member meets softball player; Veuve Clicquot meets Budweiser Light. A Mervyn's girlfriend who never checked clothing labels for fabric breathe-ability and barely got through technician training at the company where my partner was an engineer.

"If you already know," I asked, "why should we go to therapy?"

"To work things out."

"Like selling the house and making sure you get your fair share?"

"And other things—"

"Well, I'm not going," I said, and hung up.

She called back at once, which was a pattern in our relationship: we'd argue; one would hang up and the other, usually me, would call to make up. "I want to part as friends," she said.

"Well, I don't think this is going to happen. Not after fourteen years. And if we do go, you owe me at least fourteen weeks of couples counseling for fourteen years of commitment."

"We'll see."

But I knew this first session would be our last. And it was. We went to a wine bar across the street afterwards and toasted one another well. Only I didn't sleep or eat for days.

The next Saturday, I had to fly to Amsterdam for a sales training meeting. I almost lost my grip on the steering wheel when I drove myself to the long-term parking lot of the SFO Airport.

Every night of that overseas business trip I lay awake and

called friends in the States. The last night was particularly disturbing. I was in Paris and my room had a tall, gloomy mahogany armoire. Its mirrored face stared relentlessly back at me and the enormous four-poster bed. That night, I rendezvoused with French friends, into whose arms I collapsed.

Over pasta and Chianti, they soothed me. They had met her and taken our Christmas photo on the bridge in front of the Tour Eiffel five years earlier. "You're strong," Arthur told me. "She's not as strong as you. She had to leave with someone. She could not break up with you and be alone." It was French logic. But it made sense to me.

When I got back to the States, our two-bedroom cottage looked smaller and felt colder. My ex-lover—a few months earlier she had given me a birthday card showing two older ladies in jersey print dresses sharing ice cream on a Paris bench, the caption reading *Let's grow old together*—had moved out. The watercolor of the naked women at the bar in Montmartre and the Belgian marble dresser in the hallway were gone. The yellows and greens she had insisted on painting the kitchen just months before assaulted me. I collapsed onto our platform bed and cried until the tears ran into my ears.

This would become a familiar pattern over the next seven months.

Every day was gray for a long time. My only solace came on my way to work, when I stopped for a latte at Martha & Bros. Coffee Company on Church Street and the owner, Yvonne, always greeted me kindly. One day, I thought I saw my ex-lover's car double-parked in front of the café and the black mane of her new girlfriend's hair, cut in an unfashionable mullet—short on the sides, hanging down and unkempt in the back.

"You're way better than her!" said Yvonne, then she clasped her long fingers over mine. I held on to those words, a buoy in a sea of regret.

I was forty-eight years old when she left. The nights became battles with perspiration, the days a roller coaster of depression and euphoria, with little else in between. I began to attend a nearby church and became teary-eyed at every sermon. I forced myself to go to the after-service socials: the Lipton tea and homemade oatmeal cookies were some comfort. Then my dog died, kindly waiting a year after the separation before sinking under the weight of her own grief.

Two years later, maybe three, after a succession of bad girl-friends, failed dot-coms, and many dance lessons, I saw her across a crowded room. Her green eyes arrested me; her accent beguiled me. I was bowled over when she touched me. Tripping over my own feet in a Country Western two-step, I eventually learned to dance again.

Nine months later she came up behind me, wrapped her swimmer's arms around me, and led me in a shadow dance. I thought I would melt into the wood floors of the Masonic Hall. Usually, I was the pursuer. With this tall, Euro-sport, natural-eyebrow woman, I was now the pursued.

Marlene.

She called one morning and, with that cheery, quasi-English/New Zealand accent, said, "Good morning! May I pop over for tea?"

It was six in the morning and I was still in bed. She said she'd arrive in five minutes, so I dashed into the shower.

Marlene arrived, her chestnut hair gracing my doorway. She carried a large rubber bucket filled with purple and pink Canterbury bells, white gladioluses, and strawberry pink roses. With her square horticulturist fingers, she deftly snipped the stems and asked for vases. I barely had enough for her to fill. She placed flowers everywhere: on the fireplace mantel, on the cherry wood kitchen table, on the bed stand, and on my writing desk. After Earl Grey tea and milk, she headed back out the door and into the foggy morning.

After a year and a half of alternating weekends and dance lessons, we made plans to sell our houses and move in together. Before moving, I arranged with my house painters to let in my ex so she could pick up her things. There were family heirlooms in my basement, which friends had told me to leave out in the rain, but how could I do that to the jade porcelain animals her mother had collected, or the Singer sewing machine her grandmother had given her? Her parents and grandparents were gone now, but she had not left my heart entirely.

I arranged not to be there, could not bear to see the computer tech she'd chosen over me, or my ex's milky white skin.

After packing up to leave and preparing to move across the bay with my fifteen-years-younger Kiwi girl, I made one last trek to the gay district. Walking along Castro Street, a woman passed me who looked very much like my ex-lover. She was with a short, stocky woman who was pushing a baby stroller. I walked past them. A moment later, I heard her call out to me, "Kathy, how are you? This is Angie," she said. "And this is my son."

I had heard that she had adopted a biracial crack baby and now here he was—here they were—in front of me. It was surreal. At first glance, I thought the other woman was the nanny and thought, Now *you* have to cater to her!

"Well, gotta go," I announced briskly.

"Good to see you," she said, leaning under me as if pleading for me to stay.

About a year later, an old friend came to visit from San Antonio and asked if I had heard about my ex. "Her girlfriend left her."

I had waited so long to hear this news. I had hoped for this moment, perhaps the chance to be together again. The power couple, the perfect match. The madly-in-love-from-the-first-moment soul mates. The lesbian poster girls. Now that the moment was here, I felt sorry for her. Not sorry enough to call her and try to rekindle a flame that sputtered the day she told me she was in love with another woman.

I'll never really know for sure why she left. Was it her medical condition or her lust? Was it my success or hers? Was it the way we met or the place to which we had come? One thing I know for sure: If it hadn't been for the other woman, I never would have met Marlene.

From the land of the oldest trees on earth. Warm caramel wood of the kauri trees and brisk energy of the sea. Another mystery. Another risk worth seizing.

MY LIFE AS A MUSE

▼

Aviva Layton

In 1955, when I reached the age of twenty-one, I left my hometown of Sydney for Montreal. I'd never really wanted to go to Canada; my plan was to work there for however long it took to get an American visa and then, certain that a glamorous life awaited me on the other side of the border, I'd leave the colonies forever.

My Russian Jewish parents, who'd always felt out of place in Australia, had re-created a tight little shtetl that I desperately wanted to escape. The opportunity had presented itself at Sydney University, where I gravitated toward a small group of writers, poets, anarchists, philosophy students. The ideas were heady, the atmosphere fascinating, the men sexy—a far cry from the "nice" potential doctors and lawyers my parents steered me toward with increasing desperation. But it was too late: I had discovered my true nature as the archetypal writers' groupie.

All I knew about Montreal, apart from the fact that it was close to New York, was that the Dionne quintuplets lived there and brushed their teeth with Kolynos twice a day. I also had a vague feeling that it was inhabited by muscly Mounties clad in skin-tight jodhpurs who sang stirring songs of romance and adventure and looked like Nelson Eddy. But it was more than the quints and Nelson Eddy who lay in wait for me in Montreal. It was the poet Irving Layton—married with two young children—and the beginning of my role as The Other Woman.

I arrived in the middle of winter. Accustomed to the brilliant light-dazzle of a Sydney summer, Montreal felt like a hostile ghost city, its sounds muffled by thick blankets of snow, its inhabitants shrouded in layers of dark clothing. I rented a stuffy little basement and found a job in a nearby hospital. The excitement and glamour of New York seemed a long, long way off. Longing to meet the literati, I asked a friend in Sydney to give me the names of some writers. He gave me some half-dozen names, including someone called Irving Layton. To this day I don't have a clue why I chose someone whose first name I thoroughly disliked. If it wasn't destiny—and I don't believe it was—it must have been sheer randomness, something that could just as easily not have happened. A sobering thought.

Whatever the reason, I called Irving and he immediately invited me to his house for his regular Sunday night get-together of writers, painters, and anyone interesting who happened to be in town at the time. His wife, Betty, answered the door, but her presence didn't really register because the second I saw Irving I felt an immediate affinity, a certainty that I'd finally come home. Looking back at that moment, I still don't know where that feeling came from. Since he was over twenty years my senior, was I looking for a father figure? Someone who would rescue me from my own doubts and anxieties? Or maybe it was his physical presence—stocky body, mane of black hair, blazing blue eyes radiating a force-field of crackling energy. And the words! They spilled out of his mouth with such intensity. He dominated the room, his voice booming out snatched lines of poetry: Byron, Pope, Catullus, Cavafy. I was mesmerized.

A heated discussion started about Nietzsche, and when Irving asked me if I knew who Nietzsche was, I surprised him by quoting from *Thus Spake Zarathustra*. His eyes lit up and he stared at me. What did he see in me at that moment? Someone who was vulnerable, adoring, young? Someone to whom literature was as exciting and important as it was to him? Whatever it was, I felt that he saw something, some untapped, exciting potential that I'd never before seen in myself. It was such an overpowering and seductive emotion that I wanted—*needed*—to keep this person in my life, regardless of wife and family. Regardless of anything.

I can't remember his asking me for my telephone number but he must have, because the very next day he called and asked me to meet him for coffee. He picked me up in his battered old car, but instead of driving to a café, we drove deep into the wintry countryside. Finally, he stopped at the end of nowhere, turned off the engine, and leaned toward me. How quaint, I thought. He thinks he has to drive all the way to this deserted spot in order to kiss me—or more.

But no. Instead, he reached into his coat pocket and pulled out a dog-eared notebook covered with spidery scrawls. His latest poems, he told me, and started reading them to me, but within seconds the increasing frigidity inside the car made me acutely aware that I needed to pee. Urgently. The more I tried to ignore it, the more desperate I became. I had no choice but to interrupt Irving in the midst of his passionate declaiming and leap out of the car, sprinting for cover. Except that this was the middle of winter and snowy fields stretched out for miles and miles. There wasn't even a decent tree trunk. Deeply embarrassed, I looked toward the car. Luckily, Irving wasn't watching; instead, he was huddled down in the seat, scribbling furiously. I unzipped my jacket, pulled down my pants, and bared my bum to the arctic winds, positive that my urine would turn to icicles before it hit the ground.

When I managed to negotiate my way back to the car, slipping and sliding on the ice-slicked snow, Irving was waiting for me with a poem, waving it in my face like a victory flag. It was titled "Anti-Romantic." With one wave of his magic word-wand he'd transformed me from a weak-bladdered mortal into a goddess who rained her golden liquid into a parched and sterile world. The miracle of transubstantiation. "I've made you immortal," he proclaimed. He uttered those words as an indisputable fact and stared into my eyes with hypnotic intensity. I felt that as long as he kept looking at me like that I would be able to do anything, be anyone.

It was at that moment that I fell madly in love with him.

If you're going to be The Other Woman, then, traditionally at least, you should have the edge by being both younger and more beautiful than The Wife. I fulfilled the first part of that equation but not the second. Not that I wasn't passably pretty. *Perky* was the word often used to describe me. Perky and lively and bright and articulate. Betty Sutherland, half-sister of actor Donald Sutherland, was not only a serious beauty, she was also a talented artist who had designed all the covers of Irving's poetry books. They seemed to be the perfect couple.

Until her husband started sleeping with me, that is. It happened the day after our arctic drive and, when he left to go home, I lay on my lumpy bed knowing with absolute certainty that my ambition of emigrating to the United States had dissolved. Did I feel guilty about sleeping with another woman's husband, the father of her children? Not for a second! The shameful truth is I didn't give it a passing thought. Irving took up so much space, was such a large presence, there was no room for anyone else.

I found a job with more amenable hours in a downtown bookstore and set about creating a nest to counteract his domestic one. I tried my best to create the perfect Other Woman setup—cozy, but not too cloying.

229

It must have worked because Irving began spending more and more time with me. There was never a set routine to his visits. Sometimes he'd be there when expected, sometimes not. The minute he arrived, typewriter in tow, I dreaded the thought of his imminent departure, experiencing on a deeply personal level what the literary term "metonomy" meant: Irving was his typewriter, his typewriter was Irving. Where it was, was where he was. The minute I opened the front door, my glance would fly to the table. If the typewriter was perched there grinning at me with its little metal teeth, then god was in his heaven and all was right with the world. If not, I felt abandoned, saddened, bereft, even if the owner himself was sitting at the table drinking tea and smiling sweetly at me. It was, I knew, a treacherous smile because his soul was with Betty.

It was ironic that I had initially contacted Irving in order to become part of the literary community in Montreal and, by becoming his lover, became completely cut off from that community. Irving taught in a private parochial high school and there was the very real threat of his losing his job if it became known he was "seeing another woman." Although there were times when I felt lonely, it didn't really trouble me. Whatever time Irving could give me was more than enough to fill my world. The only person who knew about me, who was invited into our basement apartment, was an undergraduate student at McGill University whose first book of poetry, *Let Us Compare Mythologies*, had recently been published. "I've asked him to come round for coffee. He's the real thing," said Irving. He *was* the real thing as it turned out. His name was Leonard Cohen. He was our first and only visitor and he came round often. We'd read poems to one another for hours, taking them apart line by line, laugh like maniacs, watch endless trashy movies on our tiny black-and-white TV set, smoke up a storm, and snack on Leonard's favorite candy, long pieces of garishly colored pink and yellow strips made up to look like bacon. They were truly dreadful to look at and even more dreadful to eat. (Years later, when Irving became Canada's best-known poet and Leonard an internationally renowned singer/songwriter, people would ask me what it was like to be present at conversations between these two. When I'd tell them we watched lots of TV and ate lots of candy, no one believed me.)

A year passed by with this constant yo-yoing, although certain important plateaus were reached, like Irving finally confessing to Betty that there was another woman in his life, something she must either have known or else suspected. Although I was hoping for some defining moment—the beginnings of a divorce, a final commitment to our life together—it didn't happen. Irving wanted to keep his options open, and at that point both Betty and I allowed him to. By unspoken agreement, it was obvious that neither of us wanted to rock the boat. Certainly no discussion was initiated with Irving on my part, no agenda articulated. I sensed that the situation was a fragile one and any undue pressure would cause an implosion. Instead, each of us had our set nights, like a plural marriage. I thought that would resolve my situation somewhat, but it only made it more painful and I began to realize that the actual object of desire had become just that, an object. The real, the essential relationship was the one between The Wife and The Other Woman. Pull, tug. Tug, pull. It was a constant battle of one-upmanship, of Machiavellian strategies, of subtle manipulations, with the wife most often having the upper hand. Birthdays, holidays, the family unit always took precedence. There was a whole web of entwined lives and rituals and, as The Other Woman, I had to learn to spin my own web, to be cunning. Sensing, for instance, that their flagging marital lust was perversely rekindled, courtesy of me, I schemed to subvert it. When he took a shower before leaving for the night, I'd jump out of my clothes and, crafty as a water rat, wrestle him onto the wet bathroom floor. Most times it was mouth rape. By the time he actually left, I'd be fairly certain the visit wouldn't include wild sex with his wife. But who knew what happened on the other side of the looking glass?

I don't need the perspective of time to realize I was ruthless. I knew it then, as it was happening. There was a wife, there were children, there was a home, and I was the invader. But it was a war and I was out to win.

And so things remained in a state of stasis until the summer when Irving was awarded a literary grant—his first—which meant that he could take off for Europe. Alone, as it so happened. It was too expensive to take me. Impossible to take his family. Despite my pleading that I could pay my own way, it was obvious he wanted to fly solo. I was heartbroken. For no ostensible reason, I began to wonder if there was someone else, some other Other Woman who was getting her passport in order, packing her clothes, booking her flight to Paris.

As it turned out, I needn't have worried. Irving sent for me within a week of arriving in Paris. "Come," he telegraphed. "I miss you and need you." Ecstatic, I tele-graphed him back with my flight arrival, which was the very next day. When the plane set down at Charles de Gaulle Airport, I scanned the waiting crowds. No sign of my eager lover. None. Luckily, I had his address, a small pension on rue du Chat Qui Peche. I dragged my bags up five floors to a tiny room with its door wide open and there, sitting on the bed, was Irving, writing away furiously. He waved at me to sit down on the bed until he'd finished and then triumphantly started reading his latest poem. It was called "The Day Aviva Came to Paris." "I've made you immortal again, you lucky girl," he exclaimed when he came to the end. "And if you stay with me, I'll make you immortal again and again." I loved the poem—how could I not—but a small, insistent voice that I tried my best to ignore kept whispering that, given the choice, I'd choose mortal happiness over immortal glory every time.

We had a wonderful time that summer, crammed full of adventures, mishaps, fun, and, for Irving, some great poetry writing. For me, two seemingly trivial but pivotal moments stand out from that trip: One was the first time

I noticed Irving staring at another woman with exactly that same intimate look I thought was reserved only for me; the other was waking up early one morning in Venice and glancing at Irving's sleeping face. It was covered with dancing golden motes that were reflected from the canal below our bedroom window. Suddenly, I saw the vulnerable boy in the boastful man and my heart turned over with tenderness. Despite my misgivings, despite the warning signs, I knew that this was the man I wanted to live with for the rest of my life.

It wasn't until we were on the ship coming home that I brought up the possibility of our relationship being resolved. I'd left Montreal as The Other Woman; it was time to return as The Wife. I had a very practical reason, too: I'd landed a great job teaching literature at a private school and I didn't want to be in a vulnerable position. To my delight and surprise, Irving agreed.

Since divorces were expensive—and, anyway, Betty didn't want to give him one (or so Irving claimed and I accepted)—we decided I'd get my name legally changed to his. We'd even have a little wedding party, just the bride, the groom, and Leonard, our best man. First we'd buy the wedding ring at an arty little jewelry shop on Mountain Street and then go to La Tour Eiffel for a celebratory supper: champagne, pâté, duck confit, the works. I was a vision of loveliness, or so I thought, in a white seersucker dress that I'd found in a secondhand clothing store. Scooped low in front, it was edged at the hem with white curtain bobbles, which I thought were the last word in bohemian chic. Irving wore a creased bottle-green shirt and a grubby pair of rust-colored corduroy pants held up by a worn leather belt. Leonard, who always rose to the occasion with grace and generosity, was resplendent in a dark three-piece suit.

I made a beeline for the wedding ring displays and started to try them on, holding my finger up to the light, just like the lady in the jewelry ads. But wait a moment, where was the groom? The groom was on the other side of the store picking out expensive silver bracelets. "I want your most beautiful one," I heard him say. "My wife's an artist and I want to give her something she'll love."

I felt as if I were in some alternate universe in which the natural order of things had been overturned. Even Leonard looked stunned. He grabbed a gold wedding band, paid for it, and slipped it on the fourth finger of my left hand. "Now you're married," he said gently. Yes, I guess I was. But to whom? (Years later, when Betty and I had become friends, she told me she'd thrown her bracelet straight into the trash can. I still have my ring.)

Looking back, it's odd and disturbing that I didn't confront Irving about our "wedding," even odder that I decided to ignore it. The only thing that was meaningful to me at the time was that I was now Irving's wife. Not his legal one, but his officially acknowledged one, and I had a ring on my finger to prove it. Betty took eight-year-old Naomi and moved to San Francisco. Twelve-year-old Max moved in with us. Ten years later, our son David was born.

Thirteen years after that, I left Irving. More to the point, within a month of my becoming The Wife and moving into a larger apartment, another Other Woman came onto the scene. Whether she'd been waiting in the wings or had materialized out of thin air, I never found out. What I did find out, however, was that the triangle was an essential part of Irving's emotional geometry.

The obvious question I've asked myself, and been asked, is why I stayed for so long. The answer is mired in ambiguity and ambivalence. Over the years, I'd made numerous half-hearted attempts to separate, but I always returned. Obviously, there were myriad reasons, but the overriding one for me was Irving's ability to transform the mundane into poetry. I know it sounds melodramatic, even precious, but for me it was an addictive experience. Nothing was trivial, neither a fly, nor a grain of sand, nor any stray remark I might make. Everything was grist for his mill and it lent an importance and significance to my life that I was reluctant—and scared—to relinquish.

I later came to understand the glaringly obvious fact that no one can give your life meaning except yourself. I also came to understand that being Irving's wife, whether officially sanctioned or not, was an impossibility. All of his partners, both before and after me, were Other Women; his only true wife was his work. The knot in his life, the one he couldn't unravel, was that he was an extraordinary man who longed for the comforts of ordinary life. For him, the two couldn't be reconciled without a huge price to be paid, and both of us paid it. Irving, because he went on to have relationships with other women, all of which ended badly; I, because I was caught up in the same error: I wanted to have the thrills without the spills.

It took meeting and falling in love with another man—now my husband—to realize that the old dynamic that had kept Irving and me together for so long was losing its hold: if I were to survive emotionally, what I had thought of as the unbreakable bond between us had to be broken.

Irving stared at me in disbelief when I told him I was leaving. "But after all we've gone through, you won't be with me when King Gustav summons me to Stockholm!"

I never did get to Stockholm and, sadly, neither did Irving, though in my opinion he richly deserved to. In January 2006, he died in a Montreal nursing home at the age of ninety-three, in the end stages of Alzheimer's. The last time I visited him there, he looked at me with those hypnotic blue eyes that still flashed sparks of their former fire, and said wistfully, "We had fun together, didn't we?"

Yes we did, Irving. Yes, we did.

THE LOST CITY OF LOVE

▼

Diana Abu-Jaber

I was beginning to recognize her silhouette, the shape of her shadow.

Her.

Gliding past my office door as I consulted with a student. A pair of level eyes, dark as obsession. I never knew exactly when I'd see her.

It all began years ago, at a college I no longer teach at, in a town I no longer live in. It was early in the school year and relatively early in my academic career. I'd been teaching for perhaps a handful of years.

And there'd been plenty of others before her. I assumed she knew this. But perhaps I was giving her too much credit? Just because her eyes were so dark and stealthy and watchful?

The way it worked was: I'd look in the wrong drawer, the wrong pocket, and discover exactly what I didn't want to know. I scarcely had to look at all; the evidence was everywhere—scraps of paper containing women's names and numbers, fluttering from a place marked in a book, tucked in a suitcase, even stuck under a shoe. I'd discover the clues. He'd confess and beg for forgiveness.

When we first started out, I thought of fidelity as an innate state of being, so natural to a relationship as to be invisible. The thought of unfaithfulness—on either of our parts—seemed unthinkable, against nature. Just as impossible to fathom as the death of the loved one. To imagine the beloved in the arms of another—such a thing suggests that one has been forgotten, or at least temporarily blinked out of mind.

But things changed quickly for us. At first I knew and didn't know and hoped and didn't hope. I stayed with him after one, two, three such grim discoveries. I tried not to think about the other women, the ones he swore never to see again, never to speak to or think of again. I accepted each of his promises—stupid with hope and fear. I didn't want to tear up my life based on some nonexistent parallel dimension. If I hadn't found out about the Other, I'd reason, I wouldn't be upset; nothing would have changed. So I would simply try to will myself to forget.

I also wanted him to forget they'd existed. I wanted him to forget what their kisses were like and the scent of their hair and the texture of their skin. If he forgot them, perhaps they would cease to exist.

But she was different.

I became aware of a pattern. The activity in the corridors and classrooms settled down as the day wore on. By seven, the English Department was a ghost town. I would be at my desk, preparing for a night class, and I'd hear the footsteps tapping up the hall.

At first I'd assume it was someone from class, come to ask about an assignment. But then I'd look up just in time to see a flip of hair or a flash of eyes passing my door.

I used to ask my friends what they'd figured out for themselves. "Do you have to be faithful in order to stay together?" I asked. "What if he's not? Would you leave him?" Some friends said no, others looked horrified at the very question. "I could never stay with an unfaithful man," one (single) friend told me, with great authority.

"It's fine—as long as I don't find out," another said, with a little less confidence.

When I asked him, at the beginning—before we had any practice—how he felt about such things in theory, he would say, "I could never be with another woman. I could never even imagine such a thing."

My grandfather's cheating was part of our family's historical record. My grandmother told the story again and again. He was a charmer. Dreamy good looks, pale blue eyes, a devilish smile. She knew better, she'd say, shaking her head sadly. She was a schoolteacher, she said. She should've known better.

Apparently they were together just long enough to beget

my mother. Their life together had barely started, and one day, strange flu-like symptoms landed her in the hospital. There, she discovered she had syphilis.

By the time Gram was released, Grandpa Eddie had run off with the mother of one of her second-graders. He'd also taken all their valuables and stripped the meager bank accounts bare. This happened toward the end of the Depression. All she had left to go on was her job. She moved herself and her baby back in with her parents and that was it for Gram and men.

By the time I came along, this was to be the refrain of my childhood: Men are trouble. Untrustworthy, crafty, shiftless. "Have your fun, but don't trust 'em," Gram said.

She spoke of her own Other Woman, the mother of her student, with surprise and hurt. It was as if she were saying Eddie's behavior was despicable but typical—that's what men do! But the other woman's behavior struck her, at some level, as the deeper betrayal.

Indeed, my grandmother went on to lead her life in a society of women. Her friendships with women—her sisters, neighbors, daughter, and granddaughters—came to form the emotional core of her life.

A month or so after I first noticed her haunting the corridor, a note appeared under my office door. I'd actually stepped on it on my way in and was sitting at my desk, working, before I noticed the scrap of paper with my footprint on it. By that time I'd started to suspect he was cheating again. I'd developed a second sense for it. He was out late and I found myself writing in my journal: *I think he's out with another woman again.*

I wrote these words in a sort of disembodied state of mind. The words *Now what?* floated at the back of my head.

The note on the floor was a folded sheet of lined loose-leaf paper. I picked it up. It said, *He loves* me.

I thought, *Uh-oh.*

Students often slide homework assignments, requests for meetings, poems, and photographs under one's door. Over my years of teaching, I've also received religious tracts, *New Yorker* cartoons, news clippings, recommendation forms, doctors' notes; once, someone gave me a silk purse shaped like an envelope.

But this note was something new. *He loves* me. Was there ever a more succinct summation of the war between Other Woman and Wife?

The thing about being a professor is that, for a semester or two at a time, you're like the world's littlest celebrity. You move among a society of young people who, for a very short time, know who you are. Some faculty thrive on the attention. Our local paper ran an article on affairs between students and professors, and revealed, to no one's surprise, that such illicit liaisons were rampant. The detail in the article that made the strongest impression on me was that the vast majority of my male colleagues in the English Department were on second (or third) marriages—wed to former students.

It seemed classrooms gave faculty a hunting ground for fresh romance. The article didn't discuss what was supposed to happen when both of you were faculty and the Other Woman wanted you for her thesis advisor.

Okay, so that wasn't the case this time around. But not too far from it. He and I met in graduate school. The first Other Woman to enter my life was a fellow grad student named Betsy. I discovered later on that there'd been others even before *her*, but Betsy felt like my first true betrayal. The first time I could envision the Other Woman, and wonder: How could she do this to me?

We weren't really friends—we'd only met once or twice before. Why should I have expected her to have any concern for my feelings? But I did. After all, we were both women.

Usually, I didn't deal directly with the Others. There was only the discovery of their leavings, clues like artifacts from a mythological race—the Lost City of Atlantis. The Lost City of Love.

I kept that note with me all day, burning a hole, so to speak, through my book bag. I took it to meetings and to teach my classes. And I generally behaved (as best I could) as if my interior universe had not once again exploded into flames.

That night, I checked into a hotel. Exhausted myself with crying. I called him late that evening to let him know where I was. I told him about the note.

He denied everything. Vehemently.

He was outraged, he said—*outraged*—that I'd let what

was obviously some obsessed troublemaker come between us. "Sometimes I don't think I'll ever be able to make you happy," he said wearily. He said that a lot.

I returned home the next morning. It was easier, in the short run, to believe reassurances. Easier than trying to understand what this note was telling me.

Ironically, my father had also warned me: Men weren't to be trusted. My immigrant father viewed all men, especially Americans, as predators. He'd grown up in a traditional, patriarchal society where mothers ruled the home life and the young women were stashed away behind veils and protocols of modesty.

He was appalled by what he considered the laxity of American morals—drugs and hippies, free love and feminism. When I was six, he demanded to know if I was planning to burn my bra. "Yes!" I proclaimed, suddenly eager to get ahold of a training bra to torch.

"Don't ever trust a boy," he told me over and over again. "They want one thing, that's all." In Jordan, he could've held my virtue hostage and hand-picked my future husband. In America, it was harder to exert such control.

Instead, he resorted to scare tactics, practically echoing my grandmother verbatim. The greatest irony, of course, was that my grandmother was busy warning us to be on the lookout for dashing, seductive "foreigners." Like the one who stole her daughter.

*　　*　　*

Notes began to appear under my office door with some regularity—about one or two a month—and occasionally they were folded and tucked in my department mailbox. Always just one line, often in question form: *Why do you stay with him? Why don't you leave?* Over time, they became more neutral, almost metaphysical. *Who are you?* asked one note. *Why are you even in my life?* asked another.

I read each note with a growing sense of annoyance and dread. And then I showed each one to him. He'd say they were obviously nonsense, some sort of malicious prank. But after a couple of months of these missives, he told me that one of his students confessed that she had a crush on him. He said she'd come to his office and practically thrown herself on him, but he'd sent her away with a scolding. In fact, he said, now getting really steamed, by saving her notes and showing them to him, I was needlessly upsetting both of us, and perpetuating the grief and injury she caused. It seems that I let myself believe him: in my own defense, all I can say is that I must've felt desperate to have been so gullible.

The next time I received a note, I reported it to campus security. I felt silly and alarmist doing so, but I was sick of the intrusion. I wanted to be allowed to have my relationship problems in peace. For several weeks a security officer made regular passes by my office door. The notes stopped.

Voice messages began instead.

These were just as crypto-revealing as the notes. Often simply, "Hello, Diana, Diana, Diana," or "I'm thinking about you." The caller's voice was young, with a certain hard undertone; she delivered her messages in a skin-crawling lilt, a kind of too-friendly dare. At that school, at that time, our office phones had nothing like caller ID, so about once a week I'd hear the familiar yet anonymous voice calling with her latest weird utterance. After several such messages, she apparently tired of dreaming up new thought-fragments and the messages switched to record-ings of crackling, soundtrack-style music, usually a sort of faux-jazz and neo-classical. At first I'd listen to the whole recording, wondering if the voice would come back and say more. But the melodies just went on and on until the phone cut her off, which, on the office line, took several minutes. Eventually I learned to hang up as soon as I heard the opening notes of her theme music.

I had him come to my office; he listened to the mes-sages. He claimed he wasn't certain if this was the voice of the student or not. He'd barely talked with her, he said. He couldn't really say for certain.

But I was starting to come to my own conclusions. After six months of watching this mystery girl misting past my office door, I had an idea of the caller's face. Her image came to me in pieces—eyes, hair, high heels—like a ransom note cut out of magazines. I knew her and yet had no idea who she was. I thought I'd spotted her in the sea of students in the corridor between classes, or in the back of the campus bookstore. But I was never certain enough to approach her. I had no proof, no real evidence at all, that the girl in the hall was the girl of the phone and the girl of the letters. Perhaps they were all different people. For a time, it felt as if the world were teeming with Other Women.

After a lifetime of parental warnings, it seemed that my parents had it all wrong. It wasn't only the men who couldn't be trusted.

I told almost no one. There was too much to explain. Too much of his history of infidelity attached to the story. If that past of broken promises hadn't been in place, these intrusions might've been easier to ignore. And he swore he'd turned over a new leaf. For the third or fourth time we were attempting a fragile new start. Just as troubling to me as his checkered past was the weight of my own lingering suspicions—was this really just an unrequited crush? Was I being neurotically suspicious or ridiculously naïve? I couldn't tell; it still seemed so much easier not to ask such questions out loud.

Gradually, in addition to/in spite of/helped along by the mini-drama of calls and letters, he and I came unraveled. At some point during that weird year, we stopped looking at each other and started walking away. We shared an address but little more. It wasn't deliberate; no one wanted it to happen. We'd reached a sort of mental, emotional, metaphysical exhaustion. Late one night, he came into the bedroom hours after I'd fallen asleep. I half-woke with a shriek and kicked him, hard, in the leg, thinking he was an intruder. Even my subconscious, it seemed, was saying no. No more.

Coming apart is always a terrible, painful, hard, hard business. But I've found there can be a great sense of relief as well—the intimation of better times to come, the realization that one will no longer have to deal with this or that particular awfulness attached to that particular partner. Over the process of the break, he admitted to several more affairs than I'd previously known about. And then he finally admitted that my stalker might actually have been a student he'd slept with.

But just a few times! He protested, as if still indignant. As if the number of sessions should equate to the amount of betrayal or jealousy or fixation.

In any case, I was pleased to think that the stalker—Miss Tapping Toes, Miss Peeker, Miss Music, we called her, once our own awful confessions were out and we could attempt a gallows humor—Miss Metaphysical—would finally lose interest in me and could bring her single-minded focus to bear on him alone, instead.

But it didn't turn out that way.

By the end of the school year, I was moving out of our apartment, so eager to be gone, to flee this era of my life. I took few possessions. A table. Some clothes and books. I wanted to make a clean getaway.

I took a leave of absence from work, moved into a temporary sublet, and used only a P.O. box address. After a reclusive summer, I bought my first cell phone. I'd had it for one week when someone ("Unidentified") left me a message: two minutes of classical music.

I felt betrayed all over again. I wanted to shout into the phone: Wait a second, here—I don't want him, you can have him. You win, I lose, you lucky, lucky, lucky girl!

To the best of my very limited, biased, and deeply flawed understanding, my parents' marriage has been a happy one. As my father's aged, he's gotten mellower and my mother's gotten feistier, confirming what I've heard is Jung's theory that, as people get older, their personalities shift toward middle ground. My parents are in their late sixties now and I notice that my mother exerts herself more than she used to. She has more power, earns more money, and, in many ways, seems more agile and physically capable than my weight-lifting father. They live in a condo building in which the ratio of women to men is approximately two to one. The men in their building are coddled and pampered and treated like little princes, but the women run the show. They take care of each other. One man lives with his new wife in an apartment right next door to his ex-wife. The three of them do everything together. Mom socializes with her women friends while Dad naps. They're relatively active—hard to catch on the phone—and pretty content, I'd say. The world of their lives and relationships has altered dramatically from a stolidly one-family home with kids to a lively communal arrangement. Something I'd never have imagined.

* * *

After he and I split, I resigned from that college. I traveled, moved, took a new job. Over the ensuing three, four, five years, the creaky music messages and little notes continued. They tapered off, but still, maybe two or three times a year, a letter—no return address—would appear in my mailbox: *Where are you now?* Or *I dreamed of you again last night.*

There was almost a quaintness or nostalgia to these messages, as if she'd gotten seduced by her own pursuit. As if, once she lost the competition, she realized she didn't really want him either.

He ended up marrying a different woman, a non-student. And I hope that my Other found some sort of happiness to call her own as well. I haven't heard from her for years now. So perhaps she's finally caught up with whatever it was she was looking for.

Whether it's just luck or chance or my own predilection, or something else entirely, I've never dallied with a married man. It seems to me that being an Other must be, at times, at least as painful as being the Betrayed. For many people, some of them women, fidelity is a non-issue, undesirable, even—but I've discovered I seem to have a much more limited range. There's all sorts of temptation around each of us, all the time. But, for better or worse, I guess I'm oriented toward a single focus: the selfish pleasure of trying to spend a lifetime with one person, the great struggle and ease and effort of monogamy.

When I left him, I left the Other Women women in my life as well. Adieu, friends, you can have him. I thought he was mine; I thought he betrayed me. But no one belongs to anyone, and whether or not to be "faithful" is a choice that people make every day. I think about my faithful, persistent Other nowadays with a sort of fond relief. I wonder if she were trying to have an odd sort of conversation with me, through her messages. Perhaps she looked at me and saw herself in a fun house mirror. I imagine she was saying something like: Please promise me it won't happen to me too—this betrayal, isolation. Please don't leave me.

But, of course, I could promise her nothing of the sort.

RUNNING THE SMALLS THROUGH

▼

Lynn Freed

Being the other woman may seem preferable to suffering another woman, but to be woken out of a deep sleep by an enraged wife ranting in a language not one's own is to make one question the joys of illicit love at their source. Particularly if the culture from which the wife hails is rich in crimes of passion. And forgives them easily.

"Ees *djong* man!" the woman screamed, pointing to the man who had, somehow, slipped out of the bed we had been sharing and was standing at a safe distance in the doorway. "*Djong!*" she screamed again.

Djong? If she meant childish, we were certainly of a mind. But how to say this when she had the covers in her grip and was holding on to them with long, red, pointed nails?

I myself had often longed to stand just like that over a woman I had uncovered in bed with my husband. But no such opportunity had ever presented itself. Nothing, clearly, was going to spring me blameless from a marriage from which, somehow, I could imagine no other possible escape.

"I did not know," I said slowly, keeping my eyes on hers. The man in the doorway had, in fact, told me that he was divorced, and I'd had no reason to doubt him. After all, he had introduced me to his mother, taken me to lunch at his club, strolled me around the streets of his city without ever a hint of concern. Even now, looking back on things, I'm not sure whether I was trying to placate a wife or an ex-wife.

"I did not know," I said again, and, for a few long seconds, she seemed to weigh the truth of this. Then, suddenly, she wheeled around and made a dash for him, and then they were both screaming down the stairs, thumping, shouting, smashing things, until, finally, a door slammed, a car started up, and there was silence.

I pulled the covers up. Despite the heat, I was shivering. How would I get out of there? Find my way to the airport? And where was I, anyway? He had brought me to the house the night before, led me through it by candlelight. See the moon on the lake? he'd said. See that hole in the wall? My brother-in-law came and shot the house.

There was no point in asking, Why the house? His whole world seemed mad to me, delightfully mad. It was the sort of madness that made sense, somehow, of my being in it at all. In its subtle shades of grey, and with him leading me up the wide curving staircase, candle held high, the house itself had seemed wild, miles from any world I would have to return to.

But now, looking around in the rude daylight, I saw walls sponge-painted in a bright mauve, cheap floral curtains, foam furniture. An old panic took hold of me, the sort of panic I have always suffered when captive in alien places. I wanted to go home.

He arrived in the doorway, heaving with sobs. "Why she do this?" he cried. "Why?"

"I want to go home, please," I said.

He came to the bed to show me ten bloody welts running down his back from shoulder to waist. "She scratch me," he wailed. "Why she do this to me?"

Until now, we had met in hotels. And even there I would often find myself wanting to go home, with him left behind, a few thousand miles behind, and me with a glass of wine and a Latin crooner on the stereo to remind myself of the romance I still had to look forward to.

So why carry on? Why jeopardise a marriage, passionless and quarrelsome as it may have been, for an affair that, at best, provided only cheap hope? In fact, the question seldom occurred to me as I slipped smoothly between two, three, four versions of my life at the same time. In the version I played with him, I was a woman run through by the romantic drama of desire—the glances, the invitations, the wine. And then, once home, his sentimental protestations could sustain me even as I laughed about them with my friends. "Our love is *worsted*," he would say. "Our love is a violent rose."

Perhaps, after all, this first affair, and the many that followed, were nothing much more than a young and then youngish woman storing up experience against the future famine of old age—a wife who, even if she had given up on fidelity, did not yet have the courage to give up on marriage itself.

And then, at last, I fell in love. Never mind that he had the bad teeth and bad smell of a Brit who considered bathing once a week quite sufficient to the needs of social decency, and laundering bad for his clothes. Or that he was twenty-odd years older than I, married himself, and quite accustomed, it seemed, to snatching a woman from her husband's arms to sweep her around the dance floor, leaving the husband to watch from the wings.

Once these things have begun, it is hard to know whose desire has ruled most strongly. I had seen him watching as I danced with my husband, seen him lean forward, his lips slightly parted, slightly damp. And seeing him like that, I began to show off for him, swirling around in my four-inch Yves Saint Laurent snakeskin sandals and the sleeveless, backless dress my mother had bought me because, as she said, youth passes too quickly.

Perhaps it was she, then, who had planted in me this urgency to grab what I could while the blood still ran strong. I don't know. She herself would have been nothing but alarmed by the ever-deepening danger into which I kept putting myself. She would have cautioned me, scolded me. But, once broken, the vow of fidelity seemed to urge me on, mocking caution. I could not bear the thought of a life spent repeating itself in virtue. Everything I saw and read cried out against it, even an old woman on a beach, lamenting, "I have had two husbands and thirteen lovers, and I only regret the ones I turned down."

I can't remember now where we were that night of dancing. Austria? Switzerland? What I do remember is that we were at a conference, and that, the next day, he managed to slip into the seat next to mine on the bus before my husband could get there. And that I fell into what I can only think of now as a trance. On and on we talked, his small eyes trained on mine, and on my mouth, on my words themselves. If I said something that engaged him, he took my hand and raised it to his lips. And although I could have known how much practice had gone into all of this, still there were tears in his eyes when I said goodbye. And again when I met him a few months later at the airport.

He had come to see me on the pretext of donating sperm to a sperm bank run by one of his colleagues. Over the next few years, we met on every sort of pretext, his and mine. "Permit me to arrange it," he would say. And so I did, charmed to have the details of deception lifted so easily from my shoulders. (Some years later, sitting around a table with a group of women friends, I asked if anyone could suggest what a man could say to make himself irresistible. Everyone had something to offer, mostly predictable things—protestations of love, promises of money. And then one woman sat forward and said, " 'Leave it to me.' All he needs to say is that and I'd follow him anywhere.")

For almost two years, I permitted him to arrange my life. We would meet here or there, and, when we couldn't, we wrote letters. Oh, those years of letters! Not only his, but all of theirs. Only after my divorce did I fish them out of their hiding place—a file I'd marked *Rabelais*—and put them into a box, and the box on a shelf in my garage. And then, one day, when I went to take them out, wanting to read through all those years again, I found that the box was soaked in rat urine. So I put on a pair of rubber gloves and threw it into the garbage can.

With it went the letter that had brought things to an end. The finale itself began with his trip to Australia. Would I give him the happiness of a week in Tahiti en route? he had asked as we sipped wine, looking out over Lake Cumberland. All I had to do was to book myself on the same flight as his; I could leave the rest to him.

But I could think of no further pretexts for leaving home, certainly not a few weeks after returning. And anyway, I didn't want to. Dividing my life between home and lover had become a rhythm I counted on. And even though this was an affair like no other I had had—an affair that nothing, it seemed, could undo, not even when he'd come into the bathroom the night before, dangling a pair of greying Jockeys over my head as I sat in the bath, to ask if I'd run his smalls through—even so, I was not ready to go to Tahiti with him.

It was unusual for him to ask anything more than once, but this time he did. "Impossible?" he said, smiling. "Is that quite final?"

Well yes, it was. It was as final as my refusal to wash his underwear in my bathwater or anywhere else. Running the smalls through may have been what wives were expected to do, wives who were years away from being swept around a dance floor, worlds away from being asked to give a man the happiness of a week in Tahiti.

When he spoke of his wife, he did so casually, as if she were understood between us—Marjorie this, Marjorie that. Still, he asked, would I consider permitting him to set me up in a house on the English coast? Would I consider giving him that happiness?

Well no, I would not. Even in love, I was not stupid. And yet I did not think beyond the suggestion itself to the sort of man who would make it—a man who would remove a woman from her marriage only to stash her within reach of his own wife. His Marjorie. Had I given this thought, I would probably have put the matter down to the decades and cultures between us. Perhaps, after all, it was the decades and cultures that, until now, had exempted him from the natural mistrust with which I assaulted all other men in my life. Before and after him, mistrust of men could take possession of my breathing in a moment, transforming me into an inferno of suspicion and accusation. With him, however, it only crept in as I began to wonder why a pale-skinned Brit, lover of ancient places, cobbled streets, and cold, damp weather would want to spend a week in Tahiti on his own.

I took to observing him, listening for contradictions, asking questions, trying to catch him out. But he was leagues ahead of me in this game. "Darling," he would say, "don't demean yourself in this way." "Darling," he would say, "would you be happier if I didn't go?"

And then, one evening, I noticed an airmail envelope in the inside pocket of his jacket. As soon as he was out of the room, I slipped it out—a handwritten address, a Hong Kong stamp. Quickly I pulled out the letter and opened it. And there, in bold green ink, was the word *Darling!*

"What are you doing?" He stood in the doorway, quite still.

I hadn't heard this tone from him before. I hadn't seen his colour rise in anger either. "Who is this letter from?" I said, gripping it tight.

He walked over to me and held out his hand. "This is unworthy," he said.

But my own colour was rising now. "Who is it from?" I shouted, stuffing it into my pocket.

"It's from Marjorie," he said, keeping his eyes from mine.

"She's in Hong Kong? You're a *liar!*"

He bowed his head then. Old or *djong*, men are far more practised in silence than women, certainly when no answer will serve.

"Who is she?"

"Don't shout, please."

But already it was as if I had only a few words left. Already he was beginning to pull out drawers, put his clothes on the bed.

"Who?"

"My secretary," he said, almost inaudibly.

And then something in the grey head bowed, the greying shirt and the secretary's green ink had me rolling out the sort of noirish laugh of film that goes with lines of outrage not one's own. And even as I shouted at him, a woman longing to be restored to her own blindness, I understood how old was the farce in which I was taking part.

And when, some years later, divorced myself, I met him for lunch, thinking, "Now, surely, I shall ask myself what ever I saw in him," I was stopped at the sight of him. There he was, the grey charmer, rising to greet me with tears in his eyes. "Permit me," he said, and, "Would you give me the pleasure?" And anyone could see, even a woman heady now with the riotous, licit romp following marriage itself, that reason itself knows nothing of the heart.

ABOUT THE CONTRIBUTORS

Diana Abu-Jaber

Diana Abu-Jaber's *Crescent* won the PEN Center Award for Literary Fiction, Before Columbus Foundation American Book Award, and was a *Christian Science Monitor* Notable Book of the Year. *The Language of Baklava* was a Borders Original Voices selection and was nominated for a Quill Award. *Arabian Jazz* won the Oregon Book Award. She has taught at the University of Michigan, University of Oregon, UCLA, University of Miami, and is Writer-in-Residence at Portland State University. Her work has appeared in such publications as *The New York Times*, *Ms.*, *Salon*, *Gourmet*, *Good Housekeeping*, and *The Nation*.

Kathleen Archambeau

Kathleen Archambeau is author of *Climbing the Corporate Ladder in High Heels*. Her work has been highlighted in *Forbes.com*, *Dallas Morning News*, *New Jersey Record*, and *Miami Herald*, and she has received numerous fiction awards. A Friend of the San Francisco Library, she contributed to the building of the largest gay and lesbian collection in the world. She serves on the board of directors of a local child-care center and is an adjunct faculty member at the University of San Francisco.

Gayle Brandeis

Gayle Brandeis is the author of *Fruitflesh: Seeds of Inspiration for Women Who Write*, *The Book of Dead Birds: A Novel*, which was awarded the Bellwether Prize for Fiction in Support of a Literature of Social Change, and, most recently, *Self Storage: A Novel*. Gayle was given *The Writer* magazine's 2004 Writer Who Makes a Difference Award, a Barbara Mandigo Kelley Peace Poetry Award, and the QPB/Story Magazine Short Story Award, among other honors. Ms. Brandeis lives in southern California with her family.

Susan Cheever

Susan Cheever is author of *American Bloomsbury: The Lives of Louisa May Alcott, Ralph Waldo Emerson, Margaret Fuller, Nathaniel Hawthorne and Henry David Thoreau in Concord, Massachusetts from 1840 to 1868*. Other nonfiction includes *Home Before Dark: A Biographical Memoir of John Cheever*, and *My Name Is Bill: Bill Wilson, His Life and the Creation of Alcoholics Anonymous*. Author of five novels, her work has appeared in *The New Yorker*, the *New York Times*, and *Newsday*. A teacher in the M.F.A. programs of Bennington College and The New School, she is a National Book Critic's Circle Award nominee, a *Boston Globe* Winship Medal winner, and Associated Press award winner. A Guggenheim fellow, she is a member of the Author's Guild Council and a director of the board of the Yaddo Corporation.

Mary Jo Eustace

Mary Jo Eustace is a familiar face on Canadian television. She produced and wrote the hit CD *Bone and Marrow*, produced and starred in *What's for Dinner?*, a hit series aired across Canada, England, Australia, and New Zealand. After two years at *Canada AM*, she earned a spot as cohost on the main show. Her bestselling cookbook, *By My Side*, dealt with the difficulty of finding recipes for busy lifestyles. She is represented in Los Angeles for scriptwriting and has several projects now being considered, including her own daily lifestyle show for television.

Connie May Fowler

Connie May Fowler's *The Problem with Murmur Lee* was *Redbook*'s premier book club selection. She authored *When Katie Wakes: A Memoir* and four novels, including *Remembering Blue* (Chautauqua South Literary Award) and *Before Women Had Wings* (Southern Book Critics Circle Award; Francis Buck Award from the League; American Pen Women), which she adapted for Oprah Winfrey and was an Emmy-winning film. Her essays have appeared in *The New York Times, London Times, International Herald Tribune*, and elsewhere. Her seventh book will be published in 2008.

Lynn Freed

Lynn Freed, originally from Durban, South Africa, received her M.A. and Ph.D. in English Literature from Columbia University. She authored seven books: *Reading, Writing & Leaving Home: Life on the Page; The Curse of the Appropriate Man;* and the novels *The Mirror, House of Women, The Bungalow, Home Ground*, and *Friends of the Family*. Awards include an NEA grant,

Guggenheim fellowship, and the Inaugural Katherine Anne Porter Award for fiction from the American Academy of Arts and Letters. Ms. Freed is a member of the board of Yaddo and is a professor of English at the University of California, Davis.

Sherry Glaser

Sherry Glaser is the author and performer of *Family Secrets*, Off-Broadway's longest running one-woman show. She received the L.A. Outer Critic's Circle Award, South Florida's Carbonell Award for Best Actress, the NY Theater World Award for Best Debut, a nomination for a Drama Desk Award, and L.A.'s Ovation Award. Her autography is *Family Secrets: One Woman's Look at a Relatively Painful Subject*. Her newest stage works are *Oh My Goddess!* and *The Adventures of Super Activist Mother*. She is a founding member of the peace activist group Breasts Not Bombs.

Pam Houston

Pam Houston is the author of two collections of linked short stories, *Cowboys Are My Weakness*, winner of the 1993 Western States Book Award, and *Waltzing the Cat*, given the Willa Award for Contemporary Fiction. Her stories have appeared in collections of Best American

Short Stories, The O. Henry Awards, The Pushcart Prize, and Best American Short Stories of the Century. Her first novel, *Sight Hound*, was published in 2005. Houston is the director of Creative Writing at UC Davis and divides her time between Colorado and California.

Binnie Kirshenbaum

Binnie Kirshenbaum is the author of two short-story collections, *Married Life* and *History on a Personal Note*, and five novels: *On Mermaid Avenue, Pure Poetry, A Disturbance in One Place, Hester Among the Ruins,* and *An Almost Perfect Moment* . She is a professor of fiction writing at the Columbia University Graduate School of the Arts and lives with her husband in New York City.

Aviva Layton

Aviva Layton is the author of the novel *Nobody's Daughter* and several children's books. She has taught literature at universities, colleges, and art schools and has reviewed plays, books, and film for newspapers, journals, and radio arts programs in the U.S. and Canada. Born in Sydney, Australia, the author lived for many years in Montreal, Toronto, and London. She currently resides in Los Angeles, where she works as a literary editor.

Caroline Leavitt

Caroline Leavitt has authored eight novels, including *Coming Back to Me* and the BookSense Notables *Girls in Trouble*. Awarded a New York Foundation of the Arts Grant in Fiction and a National Magazine Award Nominee in Personal Essay, she was a finalist for a Nickelodeon Screenwriting Fellowship and she was a second-prize winner for the Goldenberg Literary Prize. Her work has appeared in such publications as *Salon*, *Redbook*, *The Chicago Tribune*, *The Washington Post, and People*. She lives with her husband, writer Jeff Tamarkin, and their young son Max in Hoboken, New Jersey.

Maxinne Rhea Leighton

Maxinne Leighton is author of *An Ellis Island Christmas*, recipient of the Marion Vannett Ridgeway Award, co-author of *Grand Central: Gateway to a Million Lives*, and recipient of the Chartered Building Awards (London). She wrote and performed *Design for Love* for MTV Comedy Central and was part of *The Gathering*, a women writers' collective at the Whole Theatre (New Jersey). A graduate of SUNY Binghamton, she holds an M.A. from NYU.

Susan Montez

Susan Montez is the author of a poetry collection, *Radio Free Queens*. Her work has appeared in numerous literary anthologies. She is an associate professor of English at Norwalk Community College in Connecticut.

Dani Shapiro

Dani Shapiro is the author of *Black & White* (Knopf), now available in paperback (Anchor Books). Her previous books include the novel *Family History* and the best-selling memoir *Slow Motion*. Her fiction and essays have appeared in *The New Yorker*, *Granta*, *Elle*, *Ploughshares*, *Tin House*, *Real Simple*, and other magazines, and have been widely anthologized. She is a visiting writer at Wesleyan University and is on the faculty of the MFA program at The New School. Ms. Shapiro lives with her husband and son in Litchfield County, Connecticut.

Jane Smiley

Jane Smiley's most recent novel, *Ten Days in the Hills*, was published by Knopf in February 2007. She is the author of twelve novels and four works of nonfiction, and has won many awards, including the Pulitzer Prize. Her essays frequently appear in such publications as *Vogue*,

Real Simple, Oprah, Practical Horseman, Outside, The Guardian, and others. She also writes political blogs for the *Huffington Post.*

Laurie Stone

Laurie Stone is author of *Starting with Serge, Close to the Bone,* and *Laughing in the Dark.* She has written for the *Village Voice, Ms.,* and *New York Woman,* was a theater critic for *The Nation,* and a critic-at-large on *Fresh Air.* She has received several grants, including The New York Foundation for the Arts, and was awarded the Nona Balakian prize in excellence in criticism from the National Book Critics Circle. Her essays have appeared in *TriQuarterly, Threepenny Review, Speakeasy,* and *Creative Nonfiction.*

Ellen Sussman

Ellen Sussman's *Dirty Words: A Literary Encyclopedia of Sex,* was recently published by Bloomsbury. Her anthology, *Bad Girls: 26 Writers Misbehave,* was published by W. W. Norton in July 2007, and became a *New York Times* Editor's Choice and a *San Francisco Chronicle* bestseller. She is the author of the novel *On a Night Like This* (Warner Books, 2004), also a *San Francisco Chronicle* bestseller. It has been translated into six languages.

Katharine Weber

Katharine Weber is the author of the novels *Triangle*, *The Little Women*, *The Music Lesson*, and *Objects in Mirror Are Closer Than They Appear*. She is a thesis advisor for the Columbia University School of the Arts Graduate Writing Program. "The Loves of His Life" is part of a chapter of her memoir in progress, *Symptoms of Fiction*.

Nancy Weber

Nancy Weber is the author of the memoir *The Life Swap* and novels *The Playgroup* and *Brokenhearted*. A sequel to *The Playgroup*, *The Gift of Evil* is being serialized online at Amazon Shorts. She worked with composer Alexander Zhurbin to adapt the lyrics of *Seagull: the Musical*, which had a reading at the 2005 NY Musical Theatre Festival and is in development. The mother of two grown children, she holds degrees from Sarah Lawrence and the French Culinary Institute. She caters as Between Books She Cooks. Her next book is a kitchen tell-all. She sits on the Boards of Harlem United and National Music Theater Network (NMTN).

Victoria Zackheim (Anthology Editor)

Victoria Zackheim (Anthology Editor) is the author of the novel *The Bone Weaver* and editor of a second anthology, *For Keeps: Women Tell the Truth About Their Bodies, Growing Older, and Acceptance* (Seal/Avalon). She is the developer and writer of the documentary film *Suffer the Little Children: Francis Kelsey and the Story of Thalidomide* (Rosemarie Reed Productions). She teaches creative writing in the UCLA Writers' Program.

ACKNOWLEDGMENTS

This anthology was a labor of love for me, and for the remarkable women whose essays fill this book. Most of them wrote this story for the first time; a few needed to muster the courage to enter a frightening, sometimes threatening place. To all of you, this anthology works because of your honesty, your generosity, and your splendid writing.

Karen Kosztolnyik at Warner gave unselfishly of her enthusiasm and support, allowing me the latitude to take this anthology far beyond the superficial "who slept with whom" and into the world of exploring the psychology of how and why women connect with married men—or survive the experience of sharing a husband. Karen, thank you. My thanks also to Michele Bidelspach, Celia Johnson, Renee Supriano, publicist Tanisha Christie, and managing editor Bob Castillo, who guided me through this process with great patience and a calming sense of humor.

When I approached Sandra Dijkstra with the idea for an anthology, she connected me with her associate, Jill Marsal. It was Jill, agent and editor extraordinaire, who led me through the labyrinth and taught me so much about what an agent does—which is a lot! Jill, you are patience, humor, heart, and keen intellect. Thank you for sharing all of that with me, and for sharing the joy and the coordination of this project.

Mickey Pearlman, thank you for your wisdom and your humor. They sustained me through the early days, when I questioned my ability to make this happen, and through the later days, when it was all coming together.

And, finally, to my dear friend and gifted author, Caroline Leavitt, my loving gratitude. Your infinite enthusiasm, counsel, and humor provided so much of the foundation upon which this book was built.